From Topic to Tale

Theory and History of Literature
Edited by Wlad Godzich and Jochen Schulte-Sasse

For other books in the series, see page 132.

From Topic to Tale

Logic and Narrativity in

The Middle Ages

Eugene Vance

Foreword by Wlad Godzich

Theory and History of Literature, Volume 47

University of Minnesota Press, Minneapolis

Published by the University of Minnesota Press
2037 University Avenue Southeast, Minneapolis MN 55414.
Published simultaneously in Canada
by Fitzhenry & Whiteside Limited, Markham.
Printed in the United States of America.

Library of Congress Cataloging-in-Publication Data

Vance Eugene.
  From topic to tale.

  (Theory and history of literature ; v. 47)
  Bibliography: p.
  Includes index.
  1. Chrétien, de Troyes, 12th cent. – Technique.
2. Narration (Rhetoric) 3. Narrative poetry, French –
History and criticism. 4. Logic in literature.
5. Logic, Medieval. 6. Rhetoric, Medieval.
I. Title. II. Series.
PQ1451.V36 1987   841'.1   86-7032
ISBN 0-8166-1535-7
ISBN 0-8166-1536-5 (pbk.)

To Adam and Jacob

Contents

Acknowledgments

I wish to express my gratitude to colleagues, students, and friends who have generously given of their time and knowledge during the writing of this book. Norman Kretzmann furnished not only bibliography about topical theory, but also cautious encouragement as I began to write this book. Eleonore Stump sent me offprints of her substantial publications on topical theory and copies of forthcoming works which proved useful to me. Monique Canto, Claude Imbert, and Michael Leff were helpful during discussions of topical theory both preceding and following the Middle Ages. Several friends read the manuscript in earlier versions and made helpful suggestions pertaining to both content and style: Howard Bloch, Kevin Brownlee, Bernard Cerquiglini, Denyse Delcourt, Alexandre Leupin, Stephen G. Nichols, Jr., and Brian Stock. Rupert Pickens, with his extensive experience as an editor, was especially sharp as a close reader of the manuscript, including the notes. I have also benefited from discussions of points in the material of this book with Timothy J. Reiss, Peter Haidu and Michel Zink. As a reader and editor of the series in which this book has been published, Wlad Godzich has made many excellent suggestions for improving the manuscript during its final revision for publication. My students in several seminars at both the Université de Montréal and Emory University have been cordial and constructive while listening to sessions devoted to the material of this book.

In the Middle Ages, during a dialectical dispute, one partner would commonly ask another, *unde locus?* — or, what is the basis of your argument? This question was frequently put to me in heated family discussions by my sons Adam and Jacob during the period when this book was written. During such moments neither the appeal to authority nor to Aristotle or Cicero ever helped me very much. Finally, the only "place" of truth during such times was a bond of love that was being stretched by growth, changing needs, and new understanding on both sides. It is to them that I dedicate this book.

Foreword
In *Memoriam*
Wlad Godzich

"They have tampered with verse," Mallarmé once wrote with that sense of awe that does not yet know whether it shall give way to righteous wrath at the horror being perpetrated or turn into exhilaration at the boldness of the stroke. Anyone who looks at recent scholarship on the Middle Ages is likely to experience a similar reaction: they have tampered with the Middle Ages, and the anxiety underlying the awe at such sacrilegious behavior does not know whether to experience the rush of release or to cower in fear of the consequences. Why should this be so? What is at stake in this reputedly obscure and generally peaceful province of the realm of scholarship? What does it matter that in recent years we have learned that technology and science were launched on their subsequent careers during this period, that the legal concepts with which we organize our social and private relationships were forged then, that a particular conception of language emerged at that time, that literacy became the measure of human beings—to cite but a few of the claims made by those who toil in this field. After all, the Middle Ages is not a given of nature but a construct of culture and, as such, subject to alteration. The very progress of knowledge presupposes the capacity to alter constructs, indeed that is one of the justifications for the entire enterprise; we should thus greet with pleasurable excitement the results of recent medieval scholarship. Yet the ambivalence of feeling will not be so easily dispelled; it will merely underscore the fact that tampering with the Middle Ages may be as momentous for us as tampering with verse was for Mallarmé: an epoch is coming to an end. But which is the threatened epoch: The Middle Ages or our own? Or is it the conceptual system upon which the difference between the two was drawn that is at risk?

We all know that the modernity asserted in early modern times, in the Italian Renaissance, was proclaimed by its promulgators as a definite break with the immediate past and that the latter, variously labeled as the "Dark Ages" or the "Middle Ages" came to constitute the field of otherness against which all that was modern was to emerge. A simple set of dichotomies was then constructed in which all negative attributes – blind faith, unreflecting prejudice, stagnation, absence of learning and free inquiry, and so on – were relegated to the epoch that was conceived as a hiatus in the course of civilization. Even the rationalism of medieval schoolmen was overshadowed by their obedience to a Church authority that was viewed as arbitrary, mindful of its own political interests, and ultimately dedicated to holding knowledge and its pursuit under tight control. It is only with the first crisis of modernity, precipitated by the extravagance of reason in the course of the French Revolution, that a reexamination of the Middle Ages appeared possible and desirable. The impetus may have come from the Romantic reassessment of reason and the distrust of its claims to universal application, but it was quickly taken over by the very sort of rationalism that the Romantics feared the most: instrumental reason in the service of the state. Much nineteenth-century medieval scholarship was concerned with the legitimation of existing or emergent states as the culmination of national aspirations traced to their putative origins in the Middle Ages. Although philology was its method, a literary history in the service of nationalism was its ultimate motor. The rising vernacular societies and their cultures were privileged over the common font of Latin learning. Since interest was focused on the erection of boundaries within the latter, little attention was paid to the relations it maintained at its own boundaries with the rich cultures of Islam, Judaism and the Greek-speaking East.

Medieval scholarship in this century has corrected this process. It has become far more attentive to the inner complexities of medieval culture and, most recently, has pursued a line of inquiry that seems motivated by the following string of syllogisms. If indeed the culture of early modern times marks such an abrupt departure from what preceded it, then this rupture must have had its seeds in the culture of the Middle Ages. Yet, if that is the case, we do not have a break but a more or less orderly development from the Middle Ages to early modern times. Since however these two appellations can be maintained only if the notion of an abyss between the periods they designate is preserved, either we have to reposition the abyss at some earlier historical juncture than the conventional middle or end of the fifteenth century or we must abandon the distinction altogether.

The second course is unpalatable for many reasons, not the least of which has to do with the rather considerable institutional investment in medievalism (insti tutes, conferences, grants, chairs, scholarships, journals, and so on). Even more importantly, to follow such a course would be to wreak havoc with the very basis of the organization of knowledge in the humanities, that is, the ability to define historical constructs as territories of inquiry. And since this very mode of inquiry is characteristic of modernity, it would threaten the latter at a time when it is already coming under considerable pressure from postmodernism. An unstated consensus has thus slowly been emerging: the boundaries of the Middle Ages should be reexamined in such a way as not to disturb the general edifice of which the Middle Ages turns out to be a keystone.

The location of the new boundary thus involves two sets of stakes: a renegotiation of the beginnings of modernity with respect to that which precedes it and an alteration in the relation of the forces that determine the tracing of such a boundary. History, as a discipline, played the major role in the determination of the limits of the older construct: it pointed to "historical" events, such as the fall of Constantinople or the great discoveries, for the purpose of distinguishing the periods at hand. It pointed, in other words, to the kind of evidence it had under control. The new boundary setting pushes this process to the extreme and sets the boundary precisely where history runs out of evidence: with literacy, prior to which the documentary evidence upon which the historian must rely is simply lacking. The emergent consensus has indeed been increasingly distinguishing between an oral Middle Ages and a literate one wherein the latter marks the preparation of, and anticipates, early modern times. The boundary is thus being set where history and literary scholarship both come against that which challenges their conceptual and methodological grasp. To say this, however, is to say that the boundary will be set where it is possible to detect the emergence of a discursive regime in which literary and historical functions can both be distinguished yet are inexorably intertwined. It is to presuppose further that we know the economy of the discursive order we are dealing with. This is far from being the case, argues Gene Vance in the pages that follow, as he proceeds to tell the story of the emergence of narrative in medieval discourse.

Vance focuses on the learned Latin culture that had been somewhat neglected, or perhaps more accurately, left to the care of those literary medievalists whose field would not encroach upon the so-called national literatures. Vance examines the organization of learning and knowledge in the middle of the twelfth century, and he discerns a pattern of floating boundaries in that organization. The trivium and the quadrivium, like any other systematization of knowledge, have always had a secret hierarchy, and it is this hierarchy that is undergoing a mutation. Since the underlying structure of the organization of knowledge is a semiotic one and takes the form of a conception of language, it is in this realm that the mutation becomes visible for ultimately it concerns the way in which language organizes and articulates the relation of things, words, and intellect, and it is here that Vance will document the mutation that takes place not only in learned circles but also in vernacular poetics, and especially in the writings of Chrétien de Troyes. The argument he traces is clear, cogent, persuasive, and illuminating of a number of historical and textual conundrums, and there is no sense in anticipating it here. I should like to offer the following remarks as a complement to his argument.

Vance notes the rise of logic to a position of preeminence over rhetoric, and goes on to show that topics come to play a most important role in the elaboration of narrative. Most present-day narratological theory has been, paradoxically for a theory of narrative, uninterested in the history of narrative. Vance's argument forces us to confront this subject since he shows that narrative has not always been what we take it to be. Specifically, Vance focuses on the way in which topics, that is, argumentative structures that are part of dialectic, came to structure narrative. Thus, instead of having a story move from event to event — a notion not available to dialectic in any case — a section of the narrative would provide concrete and particular instantiation of a universal abstract process such as the articulation of the particular to the whole, for example. The narrative would be organized around these particular concrete instantiations of the universal abstract patterns constituted by the topics, and, given the latter's universality, it would necessarily have cognitive import and thus, ultimately, ethical value as well.

The process or mutation Vance is concerned with may be usefully contrasted with what is known to medieval exegesis as *applicatio*. Here a story is told first, but it cannot be any story. It has to be drawn from sacred sources or from the life of a saint so that it is immediately received by the audience as a validated narrative of authority. The application seeks to relate the story to the everyday lived experience of the audience by pointing out its meaning. In other words, the movement is from literal narrative to tropological discourse where the latter has a strong injunctive power over the audience. Topically formed narratives do not operate this way since they do not enjoy the primacy of the applicational narrative. This primacy is reserved to the abstract universal topic which, being a universal of reason, is self-validating, as a simple logical operation can always verify. The narrative is to be judged by its degree of well-formedness in relation to this universal. It is capable of injunctive power but only as a result of a prior cognitive operation in which a prevailing state of affairs is implicitly, rather than explicitly, contrasted with the concretization derived from the universal. In other words, in application, the story's authority, which is beyond question, is rhetorically exploited during the tropological moment, whereas a narrative based on topics seeks to bring about a confrontation between two states of affairs, one derived from, and endowed with the authority of, universal and logical principles of reason, and the other merely being the case. Such a confrontation, staged for the benefit of rational beings, should have an injunctive power; however this power does not derive from rhetoric since the injunction proper is never formulated, but rather from the fact that rational beings are capable of making rational value judgments and seek to validate them through their actions, that is, it derives from the ethical dimension of human beings. It invokes the distinction between the *is* and the *ought* and captures the praxical energy that arises from their disjunction. The realm of the ethical is brought under the sway of cognition, and its existence is conceived on an individual scale, whereas in the applicational narrative the ethical has a collective dimension and is mediated through language.

The passage from the rhetorical to the logical is thus accompanied by a parallel transition from the collective to the individual. Why this should be the case is not immediately apparent, even though it has been further noted that both movements take place alongside a third which is often invoked as the cause of the other two: the transition from orality to literacy or, more properly, from a culture of the oral to one of the written. It is in this latter transition that the changes in the nature of narrative we are interested in take place.

The point has been made repeatedly that in an oral culture narratives are collective property, yet the consequences of this statement are rarely drawn out. To begin with, such a statement means that no storyteller presents himself or herself as the originator of a story but rather as a relay in a long chain of tellers, the earliest of whom, if they are known at all, are either mythical ancestors or divine emissaries. It means further that no new stories are elaborated, except at most as variants of older stories. We should expect then a waning of interest in stories which are fundamentally repetitive and rehashed over and over again, yet paradoxically all such human societies put a great deal of stock in storytelling, so much so that we tend to think of them as narrative-bound. To tell a story under such circumstances entails a different attitude toward narrative from the one moderns bring to the same experience. The performance or the telling of stories in oral societies is essentially commemorative.

This term refers to the peculiar function of memory in oral societies. On the basis of empirical evidence, members of a literate culture have a far more limited mnemonic capability than their counterparts in an oral culture. This has led anthropologists and other students of literacy to overlook a crucial difference: far less is at stake in a literate society than in an oral one as far as memory is concerned. It would not be an exaggeration to say that oral societies experience a particular form of anxiety linked to the fear of losing their memory that literate societies cannot even begin to imagine. For it is in this vast *memoria* that are contained all the sacred texts, all the foundational myths, all the explanatory regresses that provide the members of a particular collectivity with a hold on their lived experience and distinguish them from their neighbors. In this type of mindset, a story told is not cognitively processed for the information it contains – there are other ways of accomplishing such a utilitarian task; it is told in order to animate as many of the constitutive elements of *memoria* as possible. Since the audience is familiar with the narrative, be it an epic or a myth, it is not interested in its thread, structure, or even its thrust, as much as in the way in which the storyteller's performance can achieve this function of animation in which large numbers of dormant memorial strands can be set into motion and vibrate together, thereby giving its meaning to the term *commemorate*. Commemoration in such a context does not have the modern meaning of an action whereby a number of individuals come together in order to recall some event or figure; it designates the process through which the latent powers of *memoria* are brought to life. There are no individuals here, for those who are gathered at such a storytelling do not conceive of themselves as autonomous entities that have the power or the right to associate freely among themselves. They are there as the necessary material correlatives of the *memoria* from which they derive their sense of identity and purpose. Rather than being individuals with inherently endowed rights and privileges, they are persons in the etymological sense of the term, that is, material purports of roles which they do not write but accept, in the form of fate, from the power that resides in *memoria*, a power that is beyond human ken or control.

To be a person in this sense is to accept the fact that one's life does not obey a discernible order of coherence while maintaining a belief in the ultimate existence of such a coherence. In other words, if I perceive myself as playing roles that are handed down to me, I am aware of the fact that I am generally called upon to play more than one role and that there is no inherent link between two or more of the successive roles I play. At the same time, I believe firmly that all roles being played simultaneously somehow make sense, but not necessarily to me who am but one player among many. Sense, in the form of the coherence of the global play, resides at a higher level, that of the *memoria* no longer conceived as a pure repository but as an animating force itself. By contrast, persons are largely heterogeneous since they do not necessarily achieve any coherence in the roles they play. Yet this heterogeneity does not give rise to any anxiety; quite the contrary: it reinforces the belief that one's sense transcends oneself and that such a sense resides in a transcendental dimension that is at the same time immanent.

To be a person in this sense, to see oneself as assuming roles that are cast upon one, requires a conception of language and of the larger semiotic system as a set of parts available to oneself. A part is a limited ordering of verbal and nonverbal behavior endowed with internal coherence and designed to achieve specifiable effects. In contemporary semiolinguistic terms, it is a discourse. Each discourse is organized in such a way as to place its utterer in the position of the subject of that discourse, which is what we call role playing. Since persons are heterogeneous insofar as they are called upon to play different roles, we can define a person as someone with the ability to assume different subject positions.

Such a definition is overly voluntaristic however and presumes that one chooses, or has the right and the ability to choose, the roles one will play. It is, in other words, a definition of an individual assuming the function of a person. We have seen earlier that persons do not choose their roles but have them thrust upon them and that they experience them as fate. It is more accurate then to define persons as the loci in which discourses intersect and produce subject positions.

Persons are thus not defined ontologically but discursively, and their aggregate, the community of persons, is equally derived from *memoria* as the treasure trove of discourses. Objects are similarly defined: such standing as they have is granted to them by the discourse which grounds them, that is, locates them in the vast edifice of *memoria*. Just like persons, objects can find themselves at the intersection of two or more discourses. In fact, an object that is located in such a manner has the capacity to animate more than one discourse and thus to induce the peculiar vibration of *memoria* that we have earlier seen to be one goal of storytelling in this type of society. To put it even more simply, any object that can serve as the point of convergence, intersection, and refraction of a number of discourses, will have a privileged place in *memoria* since it can animate a sizable portion of the latter by enabling the activation of all the discourses that course through its specific locus. And if we recall that it is this animation that counts rather than any specific content, then the privilege accrues to the place, the locus, or, as the Greeks had it, the *topos*. This conception of topos is neither rhetorical nor dialectic—the versions that Vance is concerned with; it is discursive. Topoi are the places from which the ordering of the complex universe of discourses which is *memoria* can be intuited as . . . topography, that is, as an ultimately ordered universe which offers the promise of coherence against the immediate experience of heterogeneity.

This is the conception of topos that Ernst Robert Curtius appeals to in his *Europäische Literatur und lateinisches Mittelalter* (Bern: Francke Verlag, 1948), though he fails to trace its provenance. The reason he invokes it is, as Vance rightly sees (p. 42), because he wants to reassert the ultimate unity of Western civilization in the face of the heterogeneity produced by the two world wars. As a political project such an appeal was doomed to failure since the discursive economy had radically changed in the meantime and *memoria* had evaporated. But it does cast a shadow over potentially too euphoric a vision of dialectical topoi.

The most curious, and ultimately the weakest, feature of the economy of *memoria* is the strange coexistence of the acknowledgment of a discursive multiplicity and even heterogeneity with the belief in their ultimate, and unverifiable, coherence. One could readily view this admixture of experiential fact and belief as an ideological strategy for the suspension of societal antagonisms in view of real differences between groups and individuals. These antagonisms can be held in check as long as no one identifies with a given subject position, that is as long as there prevails a realm of persons in which no one seeks to erase the difference between a subject position and the material purport that assumes it. For as soon as this difference, and the arbitrariness that presides over its assignment, are effaced, roles are taken to be entitlements and specific discourses are felt to be somehow natural to those who wield them, and they may not easily shed them in order to assume others. Furthermore, the entire universe of discourses is no longer conceivable as a general flux whose sense resides in its specific, yet unfathomable, economy, but must be hierarchized, that is, must be brought under the control of a discourse that can account for the operations, and especially the localization, of other discourses.

The controlling discourse will be that of logic, the discourse that identifies itself with reason. It does so by pretending that it is a discourse whose internal coherence is such as to render all of its components devoid of any sense on their own and therefore unable to enter into any commerce with the internal organization of any other discourse. In other words, as a discourse logic differs from all other discourses by the fact that it does not intersect with any other discourses and, as a result, it comprehends them all. It makes them all answerable to itself. The advantages are immediately obvious. Instead of a belief in the ultimate coherence of the universe of discourses, logic provides a verifiable methodology for the determination of such a coherence. Since it appeals to universals of reason, it is inherently more egalitarian as long as one is willing to consider all human beings as rational beings. It opens the door to the emergence of the individual as someone endowed with rights.

But it also runs into some problems, two of which need remarking upon here. The first and the most obvious has to do with the claim that a given discourse, that of logic in this instance, has the capacity not only to function autonomously but also to preside over other discourses and adjudicate disputes among them. Logicians have become painfully aware of the intractability of human language on this score. Words as well as other linguistic features — and the problem is even greater with other semiotic systems — are not easily confined to one discourse; they tend to cross boundaries and to render them fuzzy, thereby rendering the operations of logic difficult. Logic has sought to overcome this difficulty by becoming increasingly formalized. The more formalized it has become, the less it has been able to assert a grasp over other discourses without invoking various mediating instances, such as pragmatic rules or the structure of the mind, all of which are but a way of acknowledging that the problem will not go away.

The second problem is even greater since it derives from the first. Given the fact that a logical discourse can internally structure itself but can only *claim* to therefore have the capacity and the right to structure other discourses and to order them, it must reach outside of itself to assert such a right. This crossing beyond its own boundary does not result from some sort of voluntaristic act, some will to power, on the part of logical discourse as we may wish to hastily conclude. It results rather from a necessity once logical discourse has dismantled the edifice of *memoria*. It will be recalled that the latter does not have a merely thesaurizing function but a sustaining one as well. It provides the animating force that brings discourses forth and, through their interplay, organizes those human beings who live by it in their mutual relations and in their dealings with the universe. The exact functioning of this agency escapes cognition in the memorial universe which thematizes it as fate. But it now becomes the burden of the logical discourse.

There comes into being then the specific discursive economy of modernity. The logical discourse, patterned upon universal and abstract reason, seeks to assume this agential burden by positing that the universe, by which it means nature, is itself rationally organized and thus accessible to its own operations. This axiom will require the development of a theory for its justification. But what is easily posited of nature is much more difficult to assert of such human order as prevails especially in view of the latter's capacity for diversity and variation. One may proceed in the topical way that Chrétien does in Vance's demonstration to construct ideals of human relations and development that are answerable to reason, but this does not do away with concrete behavior that, in this light, appears to be residual of an older mindset. Hence the project of modernization, in which a variety of means, primarily coercive and ranging from persuasion to the imposition of collective death, are applied in order to insure the compliance of the human order to the rational one. Agential power here is vested in the agent of modernization, that is, the state as the embodiment of ultimately rational conviviality.

The situation that obtains as a result is in many ways quite confused: the present is lawless in relation to the promised lawfulness of a future in which nature, the sphere of the human, and rationality are expected to coincide. In the meantime, the agent of rationality, the state, must behave in irrational ways in order to bring about rationality. In the process it may foster as much irrationality as rationality and thus cast doubt over the ultimate outcome. What is perhaps even more important is that agency in the present is beyond cognitive grasp. The state, at best, only usurps its place from the fraudulent position erected upon the claim that rational discourse has the ability and the right to adjudicate discourses.

And yet we know that discourses are being somehow organized and managed in their operations. There is a covert economy to modernity that escapes from the all-embracing claims of universal rationality. At the level of discourse, this managerial function begins to manifest itself shortly after the experiment which Vance documents collapses under the weight of its own pretensions. For in the space of the fictional opened here by Chrétien, it was readily apparent that a creative process whereby all concreteness had to be derived from abstract and universal schemas could result only in the death of concreteness, whereas the real problem was the management of the vitality that manifested itself there.

Topical writing cannot play that role and will soon come to an end. Prose, which begins to emerge then, can, and it will constitute the secret economy of modernity. The Middle Ages may well be the epoch that labors toward this discovery.

Introduction

With the surge of vernacular literacy in the second half of the twelfth century, many enduring types, forms, and codes of what, for lack of a better term, we commonly call "medieval literature" permanently embedded themselves in European culture. The extraordinary dynamism of secular vernacular letters at that time corresponded to mutations in the social order that were no less radical: for instance, the rise of urbanism, the division of the labor force, the monetarization of social relationships, the articulation of a new class consciousness, the exploitation of writing and accounting as new instruments of political power, and the emergence of international commerce.

During those decades and during the thirteenth century, almost every important rhetorical or discursive strategy of the vernacular mainstream as it has evolved up to our own time was first elaborated and contested. If ever there was a specific period of European culture germain to builders of "general" critical theories, this is it.

The impact of literacy upon twelfth-century society has been a commonplace of cultural historians for some time, though no one has been so bold as to address this subject squarely until recently, when Brian Stock wrote *The Implications of Literacy: Written Language and Models of Interpretation in the Eleventh and Twelfth Centuries* (Princeton: Princeton Univ. Press, 1983). Stock deals exclusively with the domain of church Latinity. Yet by its substance and method, this book lays an important foundation for understanding specific developments of secular vernacular literacy that I shall study in the chapters to follow. It is true that study may detect, as Paul Zumthor's has, an impact of literacy upon the workings of vernacular language and thought well before the twelfth century.[1] However, such developments occurred in clerical spheres remote from the terrains of practical political power. We may also point to features of *pre*literate medieval culture—for instance, the marks of an oral poetics—that endured in vernacular writing, perhaps as conscious archaisms, well into the thirteenth and fourteenth centuries. Once again, though, such discursive reflexes were hardly determining forces in their culture.

I would propose, by contrast, that the Oxford version of the *Chanson de Roland* may justly be considered as a testimony to a cultural crisis that was central to the political and intellectual ideals of twelfth-century society, especially those concerning warfare, as they were perceived in their own time. The eleventh century had given rise to peace movements whose goal was to limit the ravages of chivalry; the development of commerce in the twelfth century had intensified the need for civil order. Even the techniques of combat were evolving in ways that challenged the preeminence of the *miles* as *bellator*.

Not only were the traditional ideals of the warfaring aristocracy under strain, but so too was the art that expressed those ideals. As I have proposed elsewhere, the *Chanson de Roland* embodies in vivid and poignant terms the impact of textuality upon a consecrated oral poetic discourse which, up to then, had also served as the living discourse of history.[2] The first half of the Oxford *Roland* recounts the exploits of a hero who, despite his flaws, ultimately shows himself to be at one with the traditional idiom of oral epic, with its inherent code of ethics, and (what is important for us here) with its modes of production: Roland goes into battle wielding a God-given sword and certain that his exploits, which have been blessed in advance by Archbishop Turpin, will beget future songs (l. 1014). Since God, as Roland knows, never lies, we too may infer by Roland's apotheosis that his martyrdom is eternally singable, memorable, good, and true.

However, the second half of the *Roland* depicts a far less buoyant *barnage* (barony): it depicts a world of stricken survivors who no longer yearn to incarnate the values of the dead hero, because these men are old and tired, cowardly, forward-looking—or simply scrawny, as is Charlemagne's champion Thierry. Only Pinabel, the ill-fated relative and champion of a traitor, conserves in the eyes of his peers (and of the poet himself) something of the now-obsolete splendor of Roland's heroic universe.

The tragedy of the *Chanson de Roland* is inseparable from the disclosure that not only words, but even things and events to which words refer, are equivocal. The *Roland* inaugurated in the most hallowed legends of vernacular culture a new but troubled consciousness of the radical difference between the knower and the known, between unquestioning memory and exercised judgment, between the claims of blind loyalty and of assumed responsibility, and between past or present actions and their future historical consequences. The *Roland* made its culture glimpse a terrifying centrifugality, not only in the institutions of political power, but also in the very discourse by whose conventional formulas that power had been celebrated. This tragedy was all the more brutal because of the poem's failure to invent and utter new, compensatory values upon which to base the hero's quest for unequivocal honor in this world—and for salvation in the next.

If the *Roland* does indeed testify to a crisis in the discourse of power, surely this crisis stemmed in part from the impact of writing as it brought new constraints to vernacular language which disrupted the economy and latent *epistémè* of traditional epic discourse. Indeed, a shift from epic *mouvance* toward a culture of *grammatica* and monumentality is already indicated in the body of the *Roland* itself, for Charlemagne plans to perpetuate the memories of Roland and the twelve peers not by the invention of songs (*cantilènes*), but by the construction of white marble tombs that will presumably bear written inscriptions. To suggest that literacy was crucial to the disruption of the semantic processes of Old French epic is also to point to a broader relationship between writing and political power that was transforming the modalities of twelfth-century culture as a whole. What Robert-Henri Bautier has written of France in the time of Philippe Auguste (1165–1223) already applies in many ways to the Champagne of Count Henri-le-libéral (1152–1182) in whose court was nurtured the first great poetic movement of the Old French language:

> La grande nouveauté du règne est précisément le recours constant à l'écrit. On sait, en effet, que le sceau a pris une large extension dans la seconde moitié du XIIe siècle; pratiquement tout chevalier s'engage sous son sceau, et l'on peut désormais disposer d'actes authentiques susceptibles d'être opposés à l'intéressé en cas de manquement de sa part. L'une des forces de Philippe-Auguste fut d'exiger de chacun de ses partenaires à commencer par les fils et les vassaux de Henri II, de telles reconnaissances scéllées. Cela amène le roi à constituer des archives qui entre ses mains deviennent un instrument de gouvernement, une réserve d'armes juridiques. . . . C'est que dans ce qu'il faut bien désormais appeler un Etat et où l'écrit commence à jouer un tel rôle, . . . la chancellerie joue un rôle extrémement important. Le nombre des actes expédiés est sans commune mesure avec celui des règnes antérieures.[3]

The great novelty of the reign was precisely the constant recourse to writing. We know, indeed, that the use of the seal became broadly extended during the second half of the twelfth century: practically every knight became engaged under his seal, and those in power could henceforth rely upon authentic acts capable of being used against those concerned in the case of delinquency on their part. One of Philippe-Auguste's strengths was to demand sealed statements of recognition from each of his partners, beginning with the sons and the vassals of

Henri II. This led the king to establish archives, which in his hands became an instrument of government and a reserve of judicial weapons. In what henceforth must be called a State where writing began to play such a role, the chancellery became extremely important. The number of acts expedited was without any common measure with that of preceding reigns.

In the present study, I shall suggest that as a writer—a *litteratus*—and as a probable initiate into at least the rudiments of the three linguistic disciplines of the *trivium* (of which *grammatica* was the first in order of access) as they were taught in later twelfth-century France, Chrétien de Troyes found and perfected the models for a new poetics of vernacular fiction and of the text, as well as a set of new intellectual and ethical principles that compensated very well for the obsolescence of traditional epic in twelfth-century culture. Since it was held by intellectuals throughout the Middle Ages that the structure of language and its functions served to reflect, within the human soul, exterior reality, we may presume that as textuality became a new determinant of vernacular language and its operations, so too came the imperative to elaborate new and specifically textual models for understanding and expressing reality—and, by extension, to invent a "possible world" whose presuppositions were rooted in its textuality. We now call that "world" *romance*. To judge by the uses that later medieval writers made of Chrétien's art, Chrétien was by far the most resourceful vernacular model-maker of his age.

It perhaps seems natural that a medievalist should consider writing and textuality as determinants of medieval poetic art, yet such an undertaking is neither easy nor simple. Given the prominence and subtlety of theories of writing ("grammatology") that have emerged from recent critical thought, we are of course tempted to contemplate the workings of medieval texts above all through a modern prism. Indeed, a Levi-Straussian or Derridean or Lacanian "reading" of a medieval text may very well reveal things about the text that we might not otherwise have perceived. Inversely, the medieval text may very well instigate in us new perceptions about the workings of our own culture. Our age would not be the first to have considered texts of the Middle Ages as "modern."

However, given that medieval culture—whose very foundation was a Book whose letter and law were thought to "kill" if read without "spirit"—endowed itself with a rich tradition, both speculative and pragmatic, of demonstrating the functions and limits of writing in human understanding, why should a modern theory of textuality be allowed to eclipse the intelligence of that tradition?[4] If the discipline of orthodox medievalism itself has shunned studying the features of a specifically medieval textual poetics, it is not because of reverence for that tradition. To the contrary, "literary" medievalists have by and large avoided systematic study of the *trivium*, within which medieval writing was nurtured, until the last several decades, when the study of rhetoric began to attract serious critical attention and when the study of dialectics and *grammatica* began to follow suit. In the programs of orthodox medievalism, the reasons for the neglect of the *trivium* as an epistemic system are multiple and extend back to the rise of philology as a hermeneutical science in the early nineteenth century. Romantic philologists considered ancient poetic texts less as objects of analysis in their own right than as mere vestiges, as traces, of some anterior, originary meaning (whether cultural or subjective) that we as philologists must attempt to recover by a systematic hermeneutics, proposed as a science of Understanding (*Verstehen*). Schleiermacher proposed that the philologist's goal is to understand an author better than the author understands him- or herself. As Hans W. Frei writes of the early hermeneuticians:

> Both the historical-critical and the more philosophical (romantic, idealistic, and historicist) users of myth could agree with the claim. They believed themselves able to grasp, as it were from within, a mythological writer's necessary and unconscious belonging to, and expression of, the particular primitive consciousness of his era, its preconceptual and childlike sensuous level in inception, conception, and expression. . . . Where the Romantics sought *immediate* access to the spirit of the ancient myth-forming consciousness, the mythophiles thought that understanding or explanation of the ancient writings was finally synonymous with the assessment of their reliability as reports of factual occurrences and of their usefulness for explaining the origins of the traditions they express.[5]

Schleiermacher's disciple Wilhelm Dilthey expresses very succinctly what have become the implicit presuppositions of orthodox medievalism as a modern discipline. The primary goal of human studies, he says, is to understand the rules of Understanding (*Verstehen*), "which is that process by which we intuit, behind the sign given to our senses, that psychic reality of which it is the expression."[6] (Such an undertaking is conconant with Augustine's hermeneutics, which also defined the sign as "a thing which causes us to think of something beyond the impression the thing itself makes upon the senses.")[7] The proper domain of Understanding is written speech, "for only in written speech does the inner life of man find its fullest expression. That is why the art of understanding centers on the exegesis or *interpretation of those residues of human reality preserved in written form*" (p. 233). The text is not, however, an entity that we study as an object whose signification is immanent, but as something exterior to its semantic process, as a mere residue of something *other*. "The exegesis of such residues, along with the critical procedures inseparable from it, constituted the point of departure for *philology*. Phi!ology is in its essence a *personal skill and virtuosity in the scrutiny of written memorials*. Other types of interpretation of monuments or historically transmitted actions can prosper only in association with philology and its findings" (p. 233).

The originary priorities of romantic hermeneutics became the guidelines for orthodox medievalism during the next century and a half, even though practicing scholars were not always conscious of these guidelines. The inverse idea—that the semiotic constraints of writing or that the disciplines of the *trivium* (by which writers were trained to think, speak, and write) might be determinants of the supposedly inner artistic process of a text—was repugnant to orthodox medievalists. Because of an inherent romantic belief that written language, though it is external to consciousness (whether individual or collective), nevertheless bears the stamp of that consciousness, medievalists were reluctant to recognize the importance even of rhetoric as a determinant of the artistic process until, during the sixties, incursions by nonmedievalist critics such as Todorov, Kristeva, and Barthes virtually compelled younger medievalists to explore more carefully the "disciplinary" grounds of medieval texts.[8] Although the study of rhetoric has since become a minor academic industry, the disciplines of *grammatica* and logic are only beginning to command the mature critical attention that they deserve among students of medieval poetics.

Paradoxically, the first serious efforts to probe the textual dimensions of medieval French vernacular art were undertaken by a scholar who had been maximally embued with the skills of philology, yet who had begun very early in his career to seek new models of critical analysis. An important threshold in the study of medieval poetics was crossed with the publication, in 1963, of Paul Zumthor's *Langue et techniques poétiques à l'époque romane* (Paris: Klincksieck). In this book, Zumthor asserted the radical primacy of writing, whether as a pragmatic process or or as an ideological program, to modes of vernacular thought and expression. Zumthor's flair for grasping the textual dimension of vernacular poetics was substantiated in a series of subsequent essays written during the sixties and seventies. These were published together under the title *Langue, texte et énigme* (Paris: Le Seuil) in 1975, after the appearance in 1972 of Zumthor's most famous book, *Essai de poétique médiévale* (Paris: Le Seuil), made their republication appropriate. In the latter book, an observation in the chapter "Le poète et le texte" shows how remote Zumthor had become from the tenets of orthodox philology—and also how "modern," in the daunty sense given to the term in the early seventies:

"Quelles que soient les modalités du phénomène, le corpus médiéval nous apparaît comme une poésie presque totalement objectivée, c'est-à-dire dont le sujet, la subjectivité qui jadis s'investit dans le texte, s'est pour nous abolie. Sans doute n'est-ce pas là un simple effet de l'épaisseur des siècles qui nous en séparent, mais cette opacité tient-elle

également à quelque caractère spécifique des textes, à un décentration
du langage dans le pratique qui les produisit." (p. 64)

Whatever were the modalities of the phenomenon, the medieval corpus
seems to us now like a poetry that is completely objectivized—one
where the subject, or subjectivity, which once was invested in the text,
is abolished, as far as we are concerned. It is not simply the passing
of centuries that separates us from the subject. Rather, such opacity is
a consequence of the specific character of these texts, that is, of a de-
centering of language in the practice which produced them.

In his *Essai*, however, Zumthor's concern with the specifically historical dimension of *grammatica* remained subordinate to his theoretical and descriptive
priorities—such were the ways, then, of Paris (and Montreal). But suddenly,
with his book *Le masque et la lumière* (Paris: Le Seuil, 1978), on the *grande
rhétoriqueurs*, came a renewed concern to grasp and express the socio-historical
determinants of a textual praxis that would otherwise be nearly unintelligible to
us in our time. Again, in his short retrospective book *Parler du moyen-âge*
(Paris: Minuit, 1980), in which he illustrates his journey away from "le
médiévisme de papa," Zumthor summarizes his attempts to define the textual
dimension of medieval poetics, though without specific allusion to the discipline
of *grammatica*, whether as a productivity or as a mode of understanding.

   In recent years, several viable (but complementary and often overlapping) approaches to the textual dimension of medieval poetics have emerged. The first,
which I shall call the generalist-theoretical approach, may be understood as a
broad grouping of structural and post-structural analytical procedures where no
attempt is made to legitimize modern critical suppositions through an appeal to
the terms of medieval culture itself as a framework for the production of texts.
To the contrary, such procedures involve carrying to a medieval text a set of
modern presuppositions about literacy that are formulated by a science (such as
anthropology or linguistics), by a doctrine (such as Marxism), or by a philosophical debate (such as that surrounding the Heideggerian-Derridean notion of
difference).
   As does any other approach, the generalist-theoretical approach to medieval
documents influences the actual selection and editing of texts, for these operations *produce* the objects of subsequent analysis. The criteria for selecting and
editing texts have varied with changes in critical objectives. Bernard Cerquiglini
has written a succinct article outlining three major phases of French editorial
practices since the rise of romantic medievalism in France.[9] The first period,
from 1830 to 1860, was one in which editors tended to respect a given text as
it appeared, noting variations or publishing several versions, but leaving questions of judgment to the reader. The second period, from 1860 to 1913, was

dominated by the search for the urtext, which medievalists sought to reconstruct from its traces in multiple extant versions. The third, after 1913, stimulated by Joseph Bédier, involved taking the best extant manuscript of a work and correcting it in accordance with good editorial judgment. None of these methods has accepted what are determined to be variants as being valid in their own right, but rather as effects of some kind of degeneracy. As we might expect, more recent linguistic and critical theories are generating the need for textual editions that are less determined and more flexible. For instance, because of the tendency of modern historical grammarians to cling to readings of individual words and to problems of morphology—to what Cerquiglini calls *la pensée de l'élément et non pas du système* (p. 34)—questions of syntax have not been given their due nor, by extension, have questions pertaining both to the internal dynamism of a text and to its variations at the hands of the scribe by whom it was executed. However, to deal with these questions simultaneously raises new and complex problems of visualizing the text and of relating variants to each other, and Cerquiglini believes that computer science now offers textual editors the possibility of placing textual data on disks in such a way as to allow the critic to interrogate and construe these data in multiple ways, according to the specific information that he or she seeks.

The necessity for medievalists to define relationships between variants of a given text extends to that of defining relationships between a single text and the network of *other* texts that constitutes its cultural horizon. This problem is commonly designated by the term "intertextality." In a more positivistic age, critics were content to imagine the filiation of texts according to a simplistic model of "sources and influences," but nowadays we often find ourselves assuming that medieval writers would privilege and emulate this or that predecessor because of priorities specific to the later, rather than the earlier, culture. For instance, only after a vernacular author had achieved a certain technical initiation into the art of writing would he or she presume to legitimize his performance by "receiving" and transforming the Virgil or the Ovid that once would have been called a "source."

However, medievalists are not always at ease with the paradigms derived from general linguistics and semiotics, in particular with what is implied by the notion of "intertextuality." The word intertextuality was already diffused in meaning by the early seventies, and by the time the word reached medieval circles, it could be construed in any number of ways, not all of them compatible. A colloquium organized in 1979 by Columbia and Princeton universities and published as a special number of *Littérature* (41, 1981) illustrates the lack of concensus that makes medieval studies seem at times not like one, but like several, distinct disciplines. Despite Michael Riffaterre's precautionary words, none of the texts by the medievalists in the colloquium seeks to anchor its premises specifically in either a medieval or a modern doctrine of writing or of the text. Indeed, certain older polemical issues of traditional medievalism have been more fecund, in my opinion, as occasions of systematic critical reflection about medieval notions and practices of writing. Think, notably, of the famous and ongoing debate about the so-called oral technique of poems such as *Beowulf* and the *Chanson de Roland*, which survive now only in written form. Or think of the venerable search for the meaning(s) of Chrétien's metapoetic terms, *sens* and *conjointure*, a search that I shall extend in the pages to follow.

Nevertheless, the modern disciplines of linguistics and semiotics have stimulated new interest in such questions as the relationship between language and literacy, the evolution of the tense system in Old French, the evolution of vernacular prose, and the discursive hybridism of medieval texts. These have been the concerns of younger French linguists such as Christiane Marchello-Nizia, Bernard Cerquiglini, and Marie-Louise Ollier, who practice what is often referred to as the linguistics of *énonciation*, after the term of Emile Benveniste.[10] In a less specifically linguistic vein, Peter Haidu has explored the semiotic features of early French poetic texts in a Marxist perspective, while Jane Burns has attempted to approach the textual and narratological dimensions of the Arthurian prose vulgate cycle from the side of the reader's performance, rather than that of the writer.[11] Two recent articles in *Poétique* 50 (1982) treat the impact of writing on French vernacular poetics in the Middle Ages. David F. Hult, "Vers la société de l'écriture: le *Roman de la Rose*" (pp. 155–172), deals with the relationship between the *roman* (a term that designates first and foremost a language, not a style or form) and the work of writing as seen in Jean de Meung. Michèle Perret, "De l'espace romanesque à la matérialité du livre" (pp. 173–182), considers the relationship between writing and *énonciation*, in the sense that French discourse analysists give to that term.

In Germany, where philology never entirely lost its dynamism, the disciplines of communication theory, pragmatics, and modern hermeneutics have also nourished formal reflection about the function of medieval texts in their culture, often insisting upon the reception of texts as a kind of productivity and upon writing as an unending process of reading. It is through its rereadings in posterity that a medieval text comes to signify, and for that reason its signification is never static. Such is the position of what is sometimes referred to as the "Constance" school, whose best known spokesperson in the medieval field is Hans Robert Jauss.[12] Jauss's empirical attempts to formalize the process of *Rezeptionsgeschichte* do not, however, depend upon recourse either to medieval history itself or to properly medieval theories of culture for their validity. By contrast, the late Erich Köhler, thinking in a more Marxist historical and sociological perspective, preferred to raise questions about the role of courtly literacy as a class activity within the political structure of the twelfth-century nobility during a radical transformation of its power basis.[13]

After the generalist-theoretical approaches to medieval textuality, I shall speak next of the psychoanalytical approach. The great forerunner in this approach is of course Denis de Rougement's still provocative book, *Love in the Western World*, first published in French in 1939.[14] Rougement's loose Freudianism does not, however, measure up to the more precise Freudianism of Henri Rey-Flaud's more recent book, *La névrose courtoise* (Paris: Navarin, 1983). Yet neither critic deals with the process of writing itself as a factor in medieval poetic eroticism. It is in the Lacanian movement, rather, that we find the inclination to address this question. Lacan's own sensitivity to questions central to medieval culture—for example, to the constitutive role of the letter as "law" in human consciousness and to the circular processes of language, consciousness, and desire—has made his psychoanalytical writings so suggestive to those who are concerned with the linguistic and textual elements of courtly eroticism.[15] For instance, Roger Dragonetti's *La vie de la lettre au moyen-âge (La quête du Graal)* (Paris: Le Seuil, 1980) is a robust study of the "imagination *littéraire*" of medieval culture, which Dragonetti sees essentially as an extended poetics of the letter that was already intact in Isidore of Seville. In Dragonetti's perspective, the medieval text rivals—or mirrors—the unconscious as a hidden source of significations. By insisting on the letter as a determinant of consciousness, Dragonetti bypasses the romantic preoccupation with individual subjectivity that has been such a hindrance to the study of medieval texts, especially those that happen to bear an individual author's name. The Lacanian approach has been especially fertile for the analysis of courtly lyric, as Dragonetti and Giorgio Agamben have shown in their essays.[16] Dragonetti's colleague Charles Méla shares his Lacanian bias and has recently published a profound and massive study of *conjointure* (this is Chrétien's term for narrative coherence) in the Grail romances entitled *La reine et le Graal. La conjointure dans les romans du Graal de Chrétien de Troyes au Livre de Lancelot* (Paris: Le Seuil, 1984). Like Lacan and Dragonetti, Méla recognizes the primacy of the letter in the unconscious (whether literary or individual) and of writing and reading as specific modes of producing a *sens*:

> "Lettre" s'etend du support signifiant—dont l'arbitraire ne cesse d'être mis en appel—de la signification, et cette dernière requiert, en ce cas précis, que le signe soit, comme tel, pris en compte. . . . Dans le traitement littéraire de la signification, les signes sont déssaisis de leur fonction propre, occupent, dirions-nous par métaphore nécessaire, le devant de la scène, pour y jouer un rôle qui ne soit plus de simple figuration. . . . A travers les unités, éléments ou ensembles de signification, d'étranges liens se nouent, en effet à partir et autour des mots eux-mêmes, attirances réciproques ou abîmes, qui imposent peu à peu leur dessin et leur rythme et définissent une *règle* qui est d'écriture: Chrétien en appelle le résultat: "conjointure." (p. 16)

By "letter" is meant the signifying foundation—whose arbitrariness is never to be neglected—of what is signified, and signification requires, in this case, that the sign, as it is constituted, be taken into account. In instances of literary signification, signs are despoiled of their proper function and move, to resort to a necessary metaphor, to the fore of the stage, playing a role there that is not one of simple figuration. Among units, elements, or combinations that signify, strange bonds are formed, especially starting with and around words themselves: mutual attractions or abysses which little by little impose their pattern and their rythm, expressing a *rule* which is that of writing itself. Chrétien calls the result "conjointure."

Méla has elaborated on his notions of medieval textuality in subsequent articles.[17] Dragonetti's pupil Alexandre Leupin has written a book, *Le Graal et la littérature* (Lausanne: L'âge de l'homme, 1983), and a series of astute articles about the textual dimension of other genres as well—epic, prose romance, theater, fabliau, and lyric.[18] Jean-Charles Huchet's *Le roman médiéval* (Paris: Presses Universitaires de France, 1984) is a penetrating study of the primacy of language and of writing in the eroticism of the *Roman d'Enéas*. The Swiss psychoanalytical periodical *L'Ane* occasionally contains provocative notes about medieval writers, often written by the critics just named.

A third viable and very current approach to the relationship between medieval textuality and poetics may be called the historical-theoretical. This approach differs from both the generalist-theoretical and the psychoanalytical to the extent that it emphasizes study of both the social and doctrinal contexts in which medieval texts are actually produced. What social imperatives and what models of invention and of interpretation subtended the processes of writing and reading in the twelfth century? How do these differ, for example, from those governing the production of the humanist or romantic text? How do poetic texts encode the social reality surrounding their own begetting? Paradoxically, it is the very success of antihistorical modern critical theory that has stimulated medievalists to return with a whole new set of questions to the cultural history of that age, and particularly to the history of the *trivium*.

It would be misleading, though, not to recognize that there have been notable exceptions to the almost careful neglect by medievalists of the *trivium* as a source of richly suggestive theories for the modern critic of medieval texts. A few examples must suffice for the moment. Edmond Faral's *Les arts poétiques du XIIe et du XIIIe siècle: Recherches et documents sur la technique littéraire du moyen-âge* (Paris: Champion) appeared in 1924, and Charles Sears Baldwin's *Medieval Rhetoric and Poetic* (New York: Macmillan) was published in 1928. (Both books were reprinted within a year of each other a generation later, Baldwin's in 1959, Faral's in 1958.) In the field of grammar, R. W. Hunt wrote a series of pioneering essays on the study of Priscian in the twelfth century, and in 1980 these were reprinted together as a book entitled *The History of Grammar in the Middle Ages*, ed. G. L. Bursill-Hall (Amsterdam: Benjamins). E. de

Bruyne's far-reaching *Etudes d'esthétique médiévale* (Bruges: Tempel) appeared in 1948, and André Pézard's *Dante sous la pluie de feu* (Paris: Vrin) in 1950. R. H. Robins's invaluable *Ancient and Medieval Grammatical Theory in Europe* (London: Bell) was first published in 1951, and was condensed in 1967 into *A Short History of Linguistics* (London: Longman's), the same year that Jan Pinborg published his *Die Entwicklung der Sprachtheorie im Mittelalter* (Münster: Aschendorf). In 1960, Heinrich Lausberg's resourceful *Handbuch der literarischen Rhetorik* was published (Munich: Max Hueber). G. L. Bursill-Hall has renewed the study of medieval *grammatica* with his *Speculative Grammars of the Middle Ages* (The Hague: Mouton) in 1971. There has been follow-up in this field by Irène Rosier in *La grammaire spéculative des Modistes* (Lille: Presses universitaires de Lille, 1983). Thanks to the tireless historical and archival labors of James J. Murphy, surer foundations have now been laid for an understanding of the institution of rhetoric within medieval culture; see his books *Medieval Eloquence: Studies in the Theory and Practice of Medieval Rhetoric* (Berkeley and Los Angeles: Univ. of California Press, 1978) and *Rhetoric in the Middle Ages: A History of Rhetorical Theory from Saint Augustine to the Renaissance* (Berkeley and Los Angeles: Univ. of California Press, 1980). The recent book by the distinguished German scholar Hennig Brinkmann, *Mittelalterlicher Hermeneutik* (Munich: Fink Verlag, 1980), is helpful for grasping the larger intellectual context of medieval interpretive theory. A recent survey entitled *The Seven Liberal Arts*, ed. David L. Wagner (Bloomington: Indiana Univ. Press, 1983) contains good chapters on grammar and dialectics by Geoffrey F. Huntsman and Eleonore Stump, respectively. Although we have every reason to speak of the epistemic impact of writing on medieval culture, it is also important to bear in mind that reading and writing are based upon the materialities of ink and parchment that are the page produced by the hard work of human hands. In his *L'Amour des lettres et le désir de Dieu* (Paris: Le Cerf, 1957), Jean Leclerq has written about the monastic context of the medieval *scriptorium* as a place of sacred literary labor, and, more recently, Richard H. Rouse and Mary A. Rouse have illustrated very concretely the functions of writing as a organizing and retrieval system of medieval learning in their article "*Statim invenire*: Schools, Preachers, and New Attitudes to the Page," in *Renaissance and Renewal in the Twelfth Century*, ed. Robert L. Benson and Giles Constable (Cambridge, Mass.: Harvard Univ. Press, 1982), pp. 201–205).

Although the above references exemplify an increasing awareness of medieval sciences of language as a compelling matrix for thought and for artistic production, modern studies dealing with the interaction of the disciplines of the *trivium* upon each other and upon the other liberal arts have been scarce. A major investigation of the economy of the *trivium* will, however, be found in Jean Jolivet's *Arts de langage et théologie chez Abelard* (Paris: Vrin, 1969). Other more recent collaborative works have followed suit—in particular, the rich and yet searching volume *The Cultural Context of Medieval Learning*, ed. J. P. Murdoch and E. D. Sylla (Boston: Reidel, 1976), and the gigantic and endlessly provocative collection of essays *Sprache und Erkentniss im Mittelalter*, ed. Albert Zimmerman *et al.*, (Berlin and New York: De Gruyter, 1981). There is still a tendency among modern critics, however, to impose false boundaries on this or that discipline and to overlook the refractions of a given problem (such as that of "metaphor") through the other disciplines as well. A perception of the interplay, and even of the interference, between the disciplines of the *trivium* is important for students of literature, since the same processes are implicated in the dynamism of poetics of the same era.

As I shall show in the chapters to follow, Chrétien's poetics not only bears marks of all three disciplines, but also reflects above all the *dynamism* of relationships between the disciplines in twelfth-century intellectual life. Thus, Chrétien's *Cligès* may be read, as Peter Haidu has done, as a poetics most grounded in rhetoric, while *Erec et Enide* and *Yvain* are shaped more by logic than by rhetoric. *Le conte del Graal* is perhaps the most eclectic and balanced of Chrétien's romances in its manner of exploiting the arts of the *trivium*.

I shall conclude this introduction on a note of caution, which ought not to be taken as an apology for what follows. Although I have chosen to deal with only one aspect of Chrétien's narratology – its relationship to twelfth-century logic – it must be stressed that the twelfth century was a time when no prevalent vernacular poetic norms existed, except perhaps in lyric. A logically minded Chrétien could very well strive for virtuosity of narrative form in one romance and for a far less formal *rhetorical* brilliance in another without betraying any rules. Thus, we cannot adopt the same modes of reading *Yvain* as those of reading *Lancelot* or *Cligès*. Perhaps it would be fair to suggest that the openness to experiment of twelfth- and thirteenth-century vernacular poetics is unsurpassed by that of any subsequent period, including our own. Moreover, as I proposed at the outset, the experiments of twelfth- and thirteenth-century writers became, in some way, determining forces in the cultural horizons of subsequent centuries. In other words, what the discipline of logic brought to Chrétien's narratology endured as a permanent legacy of vernacular poetics, even though logic itself did *not* always directly exert its powers upon the storytelling mind. This book about logic and narrative in Chrétien's writing is a study, then, of merely one phase or aspect of a great poet's ongoing search for what we may now call "models" of writing.

As is the case with most scholarship that deals in good faith with Chrétien's sources and with his cultural environment, much of what follows remains hypothetical since we do not know who Chrtétien was, where he lived, what he read, and least of all what he himself thought. However, the intellectual competence that I shall impute to Chrétien remains very much within the sphere of probabilities of anyone even minimally embued with the intellectual resources of twelfth-century humanism. As any *Celtisant*, any rhetorical critic, or any would-be biographer of Chrfien has inevitably had to acknowledge, much of what we would like to impute to Chrétien is often warranted simply because it is "in the air." I hope that the arguments that follow will not strain the credibility of Chrétien's readers any more than do those of more established scholarship devoted to Chrétien.

From Topic to Tale

Chapter 1
From *Grammatica* to a
Poetics of the Text

That a poet named Chrétien existed, that he composed vernacular narrative poems in writing, and that he was a *litteratus* in the sense that he could also translate and exploit such classical *auctores* as Virgil and Ovid, are all facts beyond dispute. Chrétien names both himself in his functions as *conteur* and *rimoyeur* and his courtly patrons (Marie de Champagne and Philippe de Flandres), and he links the name "Chrétien" with a specific corpus of vernacular poems and translations from the Latin.[1]

Obviously, to claim that Chrétien was "literate" is to suppose that he possessed far more than the manual skill to set words down on parchment and more, even, than the intellectual competence to undergo the influence of and to translate classical *auctores*. It is to suppose that as a twelfth-century writer, Chrétien espoused a mode of expression that entailed, as well, specific and culturally determined modes of understanding both the written word and the world.

We may find in John of Salisbury, who became Bishop of Chartres during Chrétien's lifetime, a nearly contemporary (but scarcely original) reflection upon *grammatica* as a discipline. *Grama* (this is John's spelling), he tells us, means "letter" (*littera*) or "line," and *grammatica* is a "linear" art (*linearis est*). Letters are figures (*figure*) which serve as visual indicators, first, of spoken words, and second, of things. Letters have the power to "speak the words of people who are absent, but without a voice." *Grammatica* takes newborn infants from nature's breast and nurtures them in her culture throughout their lives.[2] William of Conches, contesting Macrobius's remark that the fables of the poets belong in the nursery, interprets the "nursery" as schools of the poets and *auctores*: "By children's nurseries he means schools of poets: for as the bodies of infants in the cradle are nourished by milk, so minds are nurtured in the schools of poets, or, again, so must the less experienced be brought up on on the literary authors, that is on matter less heavy [than philosophy]."[3]

Because written signs signify by convention (*ad placitum*), they, John says, are distinct from natural signs (1.14). *Grammatica* is not unnatural in a perverse way, though, because it "imitates" nature (*natura tamen imitatur*, 1.14). Poets, likewise, must imitate nature as they write, which is to say that they must faithfully represent an order of material things in an order of writing that is divorced from those things: culture presumes to include nature by imitating it, yet also determines the understanding of the object it imitates.

If *grammatica* is artificial, it is also durable and, through its alliance with monuments of stone, survives the flux of time. In the introduction to his *Policraticus*, John of Salisbury underscores the monumental function of *grammatica* in a most concrete way:

> Triumphal arches add to the glory of illustrious men only when the writing upon them informs in whose honor they have been reared, and why. It is the inscription that tells the spectator that the triumphal arch is that of our own Constantine, liberator of his country and promotor of peace. Indeed no one has ever gained permanent fame except as the result of what he has written or of what others have written of him. The memory of fool or emperor is, after a brief lapse of time, the same unless it be prolonged by courtesy of writers.[4]

At a period of history when there were obviously many more extant stone monuments of Roman antiquity than have survived in modern times and at a period when medieval builders of churches, bridges, and castles were emulating antiquity by building new stone monuments appropriate to their own gods and heroes, the challenge of classical *grammatica* was also being cheerfuly taken up by vernacular writers (including Chrétien) who were appropriating the great legends of past history (Thebes, Troy, Athens, Rome) as predecessors of their own literate *modernitas*. Indeed, *grammatica* came to be seen in the vernacular *roman d'antiquité* as the very foundation of ancient civic order.[5] Thus, Cadmus, inventer of the alphabet, was known as a founder of Thebes; inversely, Capaneus, in the *Roman de Thèbes*, threatens to dismantle all the stones of Thebes that Amphyon "assembla ci par artimaire / et par la force de grammaire / et par le chant de sa viele . . . " (vol. 1, ll. 9329–25) ("assembled here by magic and by the force of grammar and writing, and by the song of his viele").

A pupil learned *grammatica* not only from books of grammar (Donatus, Priscian, and others) but also by reading and explicating the works of the classical authors, and the lesson (*lectio*) was useless without the commentary (*enarratio*). The exposition of a given text began with the *littera*, or the grammatical explanation, then passed to the *sensus*, which was the signification of the words in their context, and finally to the *sententia*, or the understanding of the author's thought.[6] The reception of texts from the *auctores* was hardly a passive process. To the contrary, a responsible reading was also a rewriting, a production of a new meaning *through* the old. If twelfth-century intellectuals called themselves "modern," it was because their new hermeneutical vision taught them both the timeliness of meaning and the meaningfulness of time.

The mere *mise en escrit* of vernacular discourse may very well have disrupted a hallowed formal and semantic tradition of oral epic and surely coincided with a cleavage in the modalities of political power. But the formal discipline of *grammatica* brought to the twelfth-century romance poet a sharper historical perspective upon his or her inherited *matière*. Douglas Kelly has sought to define this hermeneutical perspective thus:

> Marie de France says that poets examine the monuments of the past in order to penetrate their obscurity and to rediscover, or rather to re-store, their meaning. This illumination of monuments of the past reveals, then, "what used to be" (*ceo k'i ert*). Chrétien restores a *bele conjointure* to the story of *Erec and Enide* that his contemporaries, he says, make ugly by their disjunctions and suppressions (*depécier et corrompre*, v. 21). It is thus out of the *disiecta membra* of his material that the poet reconstructs the ancient edifice, the *domus reconstruenda*. A demolished and ruined house will be restored into a beautiful romance.[7]

This hermeneutical perspective of the poet as *litteratus* marks Chrétien's discourse with the fiction of a double temporality whose tense structure differs from that in the *Roland*.[8] On the one hand, we observe a temporal axis of past events comprised by the *matière* of the story itself, whose privileged tense is the preterit — that is, the temporal indicator of a discrete past holding its own specificity, its own marvelous space, its own encoded truth, a past whose continuity with itself could be conveyed by the precise and systematic exploitation of the perfect, imperfect, and pluperfect tenses.[9] Suspended as it is in preterits, the diegetic world belongs to a documented past whose preterit tense was already proper above all to writing (and not to the living voice) even though such writing is inflected, in long long stretches of direct discourse, so as to *imitate* dramatically the living voice.[10] The voice has become the primal fiction of the romance text.

On the other hand, there is the axis of an extradiegetic temporal present (expressed in writing) which conveys the fiction of the poet's living voice as it both utters and comments here and now upon the exalted events of ancient times:[11]

> Mes por parler de çaus qui furent,
> Leissons çaus, qui an vie durent!

> But in order to speak of those who once were,
> Let us leave those who are now living.[12]

As Marie-Louise Ollier has written,

> "La fiction dans le roman en vers est clairement située à la fois dans un passé et dans un ailleurs, dissociée de l'expérience actuellement vécue, ne serait-ce que par l'intervention d'une écriture hautement revendiquée. Mais le 'présent du récit' est ici celui de la voix, qui introduit dans le passé de l'histoire le présent, concret, charnel, de sa propre respiration, institue une sorte de dialectique nonchalante entre la fiction contée et le réel de l'acte poétique."[13]

> The fictive in the poetic romance is clearly situated at once in a time past and in another place, dissociated from present experience, thanks to the strong revindication of writing. But the "narrative present" is here that of the voice, which injects the presence, the concreteness, the corporeality of its own breathing into the past, thereby instigating a kind of nonchanlant dialectic between narrated fiction and the reality of the poetic act.

In a more recent study of tense usage in Old French narrative, Rupert T. Pickens has gathered broad statistical evidence to document what he calls the "overall tension created by opposing historicizing and anti-historicizing forces" in narrative. Pickens indicates that, beginning with *Cligès*, Chrétien "undertook experimentation with more pervasive anti-historicization in the composition of his narratives," and that in *Yvain*, anti-historicizing features predominate.[14]

This hermeneutical opposition between present and past corresponds to a growing sense in the twelfth century of the distinction between *estoire* as "history" and *estoire* as "story." Stephen G. Nichols, Jr., has recently shown in his book, *Romanesque Signs: Early Medieval Narrative and Iconography* (New Haven: Yale Univ. Press, 1983), to what extent a broad new historical consciousness emerged out of eleventh century theology and marked the dominant semiotic systems of Romanesque culture. Nichols stresses, however, the teleological nature of that historical consciousness. Douglas Kelly sees this development maturing rather later in vernacular poetics. He writes, "Though about 1175 no real distinction was made between history and romance, from a modern point of view, an evolution is apparent from the nearly historical to outright fiction. That romancers were writing fiction was undeniable by 1200, and the increasing criticism of their fabulous 'lies' brought that fact home."[15]

Like the literature of most periods in our culture, medieval vernacular poetry tends both to fictionalize the process of its own begetting and to celebrate in its heroes cognitive processes that reflect the author's own. If there is any warrant for my claim that Charlemagne's designs to erect a splendid marble sarcophagus for Roland and the twelve peers signal a new awareness, in the *Roland*, of the difference between oral culture and a cult of monumental literacy,[16] so too in Chrétien's *Chevalier de la charrette* we find a hero who not only knows how to read the tombstones of his future peers from the Round Table, but also can raise the lid of the most splendid tomb of them all: this is the tomb reserved (as the inscription and its monkish reader tell us) for the hero himself as the liberator of the Queen and the people of Logres. Lancelot shows himself to be a master of the text, of both its "outside" and its "sweet," hidden "inside," despite the hermit's attempts to discourage him:

> "C'est un veissiax qui a passez
> toz ces qui onques furent fet;
> si riche ne si bien portret
> ne vit onques ne je ne nus;
> biax est dedanz et defors plus;
> mes ce metez en nonchaloir,
> que rien en vos porroit valoir,
> que ja ne la verroiz dedanz."[17]

"This is a vessel that surpasses all that were ever made; one so rich and well designed was never seen, by me or by anyone: it is beautiful inside, and more beautiful without; but put it out of mind, for you can do nothing about it: never will you see what is inside."

Lancelot's miraculous display of strength in lifting the cover of the tomb, especially in the face of an unbelieving monk, is a hermeneutical deed of the most heroic sort. However, Lancelot does not tell us, finally, what he sees inside this splendid crypt. To the contrary, an interesting displacement occurs: having opened the tomb, Lancelot *himself* becomes a living crypt whose inner secret he refuses to disclose to the curious monk. The sweet, inner mysteries of a courtly messiah are simply not destined for monkish ears. Chrétien is quite clearly and very boldly appropriating, for his vernacular story and its heroes, a textual hermeneutics once reserved for the domaine of the *auctores* and of Scripture.[18] Nor do Chrétien's male heroes have a monopoly upon the power of reading. Women can do it too, and nothing, it would seem, is more overpowering to a knight than the spectacle of a woman reading a well-wrought text. Such is the case with Yvain, in any case, who falls in love with Laudine as she reads a Psalter with golden letters (ll. 1414–1415). The letter instigates in Yvain a fetishistic erotic desire that competes with the young widow's longing for sacred consolation.

Thus, if a hermeneutical privilege proper to the poet as *litteratus* marks the primal relationship between his enunciating voice and the inherited *matière* being redeployed in his narrative text, so too a new hermeneutical imperative marks the secondary, fictive relationship between the adventuring hero and the

Arthurian world of equivocal people and things in which he moves. And through heroic actions, a questing knight "invents" a new meaning of his world whose ultimate form is the revivified body of romance itself. Chrétien's critics are unanimous, moreover, in underscoring the primacy of judgment and understanding to heroic action in his romances. For instance, Rupert T. Pickens claims that "the *Conte del Graal* is a poem largely 'about' signs and the interpretations of signs."[19] "Specifically, judgment and evaluation are involved in the interpretation of signs, a theme close to the heart of the poem's meaning. Signs, in this sense, are words, gestures, and objects" (p. 57). "His entire poem, which is concerned thematically with judgment, evaluation, and interpretation, is itself the product of Chrétien's judgment, evaluation, and interpretation of a fictive source" (p. 58).

In the opening episodes of *Yvain*, as well, Chrétien brings strong dramatic relief to the tendency of medieval narrative fiction to double its own extradiegetic processes of invention. The setting is Arthur's court, where the knights of the Round Table have gathered for a feast at Pentecost, whose theme celebrates that archetypal hermeneutical triumph over the legacy of Babel that occurred when the Holy Spirit enlightened, in their own tongue, each of the peoples from every nation under heaven who were gathered in Jerusalem (Acts 2.1–8). After dinner, the proper moment has come for tales of prowess and love to be told and interpreted. Arthur's court is a place of double abundance, of feasts and stories to nourish both body and soul. Here raw events that have occurred during adventures in *sauvage terre* are enculturated as cooked, courteous narrative. Just as the writer of narrative must withdraw from human company into his *clausum cubiculum*, as Quintilian puts it,[20] in order to thrash out the text that he will later perform before the public, so too the questing knight must withdraw from the court, enclose himself in his armor, and depart alone into the wilderness in order to invent, by his deeds, a story that he will later submit to the *iudicium* of his peers in the court. A hero's quest as a knight, like Chrétien's as writer, is to produce the best possible story. In King Arthur's court, *matière* is (or is supposed to be) crowned with *sens*.

However, if Chrétien shows us through the struggles of his heroes that the *invention* of excellent narrative is a difficult and dangerous process, so too we see in *Yvain* that the proper *interpretation* of a fine story is anything but a fait accompli, and that it involves overcoming hard obstacles in its reception as well. For, exactly at the moment in the feast when chivalrous tales are to be told, Arthur abruptly withdraws from the assembly of knights and ladies that he is supposed to govern and retires to his bed. Arthur has abdicated his duty of presiding over those festivities of food and word where knights celebrate and renew, in both body and spirit, their collective, aristocratic identity. Although the Queen has dutifully followed Arthur to his bed until that time when he has "forgotten himself and gone to sleep" (l. 52), the Queen has not lost, even in Arthur's bed, her keener appetite for stories of heroic love. Thus, when she hears that a tale is about to be told among the assembly of knights and ladies outside her door, she rises from the King's bed to join them: marvelous stories of love, for Guenevere, are as compelling as the act of ordinary carnal love itself. Guenevere desires to desire.

As the Queen joins the assembly of knights, Calogrenant, who is on the verge of telling his tale, sees her first and courteously rises. Kay is jealous, and in the King's absence Kay dares to blaspheme both the Queen and Calogrenant. Kay is a *médisant*, that is, a stock figure of the courtly habitat who constantly transgresses the code of true courtesy — or of courteous truth. However, Kay's verbal anarchy only reinforces the obligation of the court to revalorize the institution of courtly discourse, and for this reason his transgressions actually *belong* to the customs of the court. As the Queen says of Kay, " 'It is his custom to speak evil' " (" '*Costumiers est de dire mal*,' " (l. 134). In other words, Kay dialectically defines those norms of courtesy that must prevail in the social group before the world of romance fiction may become possible and true. Kay's verbal transgressions instigate courtly narrative in the same way that the *médisant's* scandalmongering and mockery of *fin'amor* instigate the "true" courtly lyric song.[21]

Calogrenant goes on to tell a tale about himself that occurred long ago, hence, belongs to history, yet one that has been previously concealed because it is "not of his honor, but his shame" ("*Non de s'enor, mes de sa honte*," l. 60). In a court where nothing succeeds like stories of success, Calogrenant's tale is deficient, not only in terms of its *matière*, but even in those terms by which he himself says his tale ought to be judged. Just as, for the dialectician, the processes of inventing and of judging arguments are distinct, so too for Chrétien and his hero the processes of narrating and interpreting a story are distinct. Calogrenant does not grasp, himself, the *sens* of the *matière* that he exhorts his audience to grasp, not with their ears, but with their hearts. Calogrenant does not see the connection in his own story between his failure as a potential lover of the vavasor's beautiful and unwedded daughter, whose acquaintance he makes in a garden, and his subsequent failure in chivalric combat with Esclados. Calogrenant has not mastered the art of *conjointure*, whether as concrete exploits *in factis* or as narrative feats *in verbis*. Calogrenant is a bad poet, and he has put the *domus* of chivalric romance in shambles. Calogrenant's audience, as well, is in shambles: its King is absent, and the pure anarchy of *médisance* prevails. It is not difficult to see an analogy between the fiasco of Calogrenant's narrative and the "disjoined" state of courtly art that Chrétien thinks he has inherited. Whenever bad art becomes the subject of good art, the problem of critical understanding becomes metacritical, and this shifting of priorities is very much characteristic of the climate of hermeneutical debate that marked twelfth-century intellectual life from Abelard onward.

Yvain, however, is galvanized by this story of shame, defeat and confusion, and the young knight vows to bring the story to a new conclusion which will restore the pre-scribed norms of "true" courtly narrative. We should note that this untried knight does not, himself, create either the story in which he is about to figure or his role in it: he *inherits* that story and he vindicates his role in it. So too, the untried *litteratus* inherits his *matière* from the past and "translates" it into new monuments, not Greek or Roman, but French and "Christian" (that is, both Christian, and *by* Chrétien). As Chrétien says in the prologue to *Erec et Enide*:

> Des or comancerai l'estoire
> qui toz jorz mes iert an mimoire
> tant con durra crestïentez;
> de ce s'est Crestïens vantez.[22]

Right now, I shall begin the story, which will always endure in memory so long as Christianity endures: this is Chrétien's boast.

Like Chrétien is by his writing, so Yvain is by his deeds a *remanieur* of courtly narrative, not only as it is produced, but also as it is received, for both Chrétien the writer and his story-making hero show that the invention and reception of art are distinct but also mutually determining processes. Yvain's first gesture is to restore the *code* of courtly discourse: he silences Kay by declining to argue with him on his own unworthy grounds: "He does not start a fight who strikes the first blow, rather he who venges himself" (*"Que cil ne fet pas la meslee, / Qui fiert la premiere colee, / Ainz la fet cil, qui se revange,"* ll. 641–43). When the King awakens from his unkingly sleep and returns to the assembly, the Queen renarrates Calogrenant's story, though only, we are told, "word by word" (*"mot a mot,"* l. 559) — that is, passively without interpreting it. Chrétien reflects, here, the schoolman's distinction between mere *recitatores*, who only pronounce the words of their "author's" text, and *interpretes*, who "declare" (*declarant*) the meanings of obscure things in their author's text. Although the king is properly stirred by Guenevere's reporting of this defective tale and vows to undertake Calogrenant's failed adventure (hence, to restore the norms of courtly art), Yvain is so determined to make this quest his own that he decides to set forth by himself, "whether for his joy or his grief" (*"Ou a sa joie ou a son duel,"* l. 694). Yvain already imagines himself as the new protagonist of each event in the story that Calogrenant has just recounted (ll. 695–722), though he does not yet know whether his forthcoming *poesis* of this inherited tale will bring honor or shame:

> Mes il ne s'an quiert ja vanter,
> Ne ja son vuel nus nel savra

Jusqu'a tant que il an avra
Grante honte ou grant enor eüe,
Puis si soit la chose seüe.

(ll. 718–22)

But he scarcely wants to boast, or that anyone should know his desire, until he shall have earned great shame or great honor: then might the thing be known.

We are witnessing, here, the transformation of a story as it passes through three distinct phases: first, what "really happened" to Calogrenant; second, what Calogrenant has *told* us about what happened; third, what Yvain imagines and *wants* to happen — and Chrétien surely expects his audience to observe here what is occurring in his own process of narrative invention. Moreover, Chrétien's highlighting of two different psychic perspectives upon "what happened" — Calogrenant's which is defective, Yvain's which is perfective — corresponds in certain ways to Abelard's distinctions between the perception (*sensus*) of an existing thing (*res*) and the intellection (*intellectio*) of the thing, the latter being arbitrary, susceptible to error, and proper to the life of the soul itself: "Just as the meaning (*sensus*) of something is not the thing itself, neither is the intellection the form of the object conceived. It is, rather, a certain action of the soul, thanks to which the soul is called intelligent, while the form that orients such action is an imaginary and fictive thing (*res imaginaria et quaedam est et ficta*) that the mind fabricates (*conficit*) when it wishes and as it wishes, such as those imaginary cities we see in our sleep or such as that form of a building that the artisan conceives of when something is to be built."[23]

As heroes, respectively, of epic and romance, Roland and Yvain clearly do not move in the same ontological landscape or think according to the same model of mind. Roland's world is one of hierarchies, and ascendance is the ethical imperative of that world; and, with ascendance, comes the merger of individual heroic will with that of a heroic God in whose belligerent image Roland wills to fight. Yvain's world is primarily one of immanent, horizontal relationships between things and people, and a true perception and proper judgment of those relationships here and now is a precondition of ethically responsible action. Like Roland, Yvain is a creature of will; however, the *sagesse* represented externally (and so tentatively) by Roland's friend (and subordinate) Oliver is now intrinsic to the *courtly* heroic soul and must govern the life of that soul.

By defeating Esclados at the marvelous fountain and conquering the heart of the dead knight's widow Laudine, Yvain succeeds in redressing Calogrenant's previously defective *conjointure* of combat and love. Yvain is Chrétien's counterpart as a *remanieur* of courtly narrative, for he has made a story complete or "perfect" in the medieval sense of that word.

However, Yvain's redeemed story calls for a redeemed audience, and Chrétien sees to it that justice is done on that score as well. When Arthur himself appears in the forest of Broceliande to spill liquid from the basin onto the stone by the marvelous fountain, now Yvain, rather than Esclados, appears as the fountain's anonymous protector, and Kay is now his adversary in the joust. Yvain easily puts *médisance* in its place (on the ground), yet Yvain is reluctant to inflict any other punishment. The courtly world proves it is right whenever it proves that Kay is wrong, and obviously the whole process of demonstrating that rightness is quite worthwhile:

> Mes sire Yvains cop si puissant
> Li dona, que par son la sele
> A fet Keus la torneboele,
> Et li hiaumes an terre fiert.
> Plus d'enui feire ne li quiert
> Mes sire Yvains
> (ll. 2254–59)

My lord Yvain gave him such a blow that Kay did a somersault over his saddle, and his helmet hit the ground. My lord Yvain does not want to harm him any more than this.

At the King's request, Yvain now narrates the fourth and final—and properly courtly—version of his (and Chrétien's) inherited tale. Arthur is now anything but sleepy, and "covets" to hear about Yvain's adventure. *Auctoritas*, understood as a dynamic but reasonable principle of cultural renewal, is alive and well, and a new hero (Chrétien) joins its ranks as Yvain flawlessly narrates his tale and as the King invites the whole assembly (including Kay) to his lodging:

> Onques de mot n'i antreprist,
> Ne rien nule n'i oblia.
> Et aprés ce le roi pria
> Que il et tuit si chevalier
> Venissent o lui herbergier.
> (l. 2300–2304)

Never did a word go astray, nor did he forget a single thing. And after that, the King prayed that he and all his knights come to lodge with him.)

In sum, the opening segment of Yvain dramatizes, through the *avanture* of the romance's titular hero, a writer's quest to achieve artistic excellence, and he has done so by running the risk of making bad art into a subject of good art. However, truth in good fiction was never a simple concept, nor was it ever compatible with troth that has not been severely tried. Chrétien's bent was to explore truth and troth together, and in doing so, to inculcate new depth and complexity to both. Chrétien's poetics of love is also a poetics of understanding. As we shall see in the next chapter, Chrétien drew broadly upon the intellectual resources of his age to make one art as subtle as the other.

Chapter 2
De voir dire mot le conjure:
Dialectics and Fictive Truth

Chretien's romances express more than one hermeneutical concept pertaining to the relationship between *matière*, language, and truth, or, in more philosophical terms, between things, words, and intellect. For this reason Chrétien's art may be seen as a crossroad of different epistemological trends in twelfth-century culture in general and in the discipline of *grammatica* in particular.

On the one hand, we find in his art the persistence of a conservative and fundamentally Augustinian hermeneutics, a mystical one to the extent that the perception of truth was above all an operation of the charitable human will that is rewarded by divine illumination. For instance, Calogrenant's claim that in order to grasp the truth of his tale we must listen not only with our ears, but inwardly, with our hearts as well, is strongly reminiscent of Augustine's theory that spiritual understanding is imparted by God to humanity not through fleshly ears, but through the inner "ears of the heart" (*aures cordis, Confessions* 1. 5). For Augustine, it is the human capacity for spiritual understanding that sets men and women apart from the human as mere animal (*homo animalis*), the latter being capable only of corporeal perception. Spiritual knowledge is bestowed by the Holy Spirit upon the charitable soul. Charity is attained through will. It is plausible to see Perceval's sinful refusal to ask the Grail's meaning in the castle of the Roi Pescheor as a failure of will and charity in understanding. Such is the tenor of the response of the hermit to whom Perceval has just confessed:

> "Peschie[z] la langue te trencha
> Quant le fer qui onc n'estancha

Se sainier devant toi veïs,"
Ne la raison n'en enqueïs.
Et quant del graal ne sëus
Cui l'en en sert, fol sens eüs."[1]

"Sin cut off your tongue when you saw before you the lance that never stopped bleeding, and you did not ask its meaning. And when you did not learn who is served from the grail, this was folly."

On the other hand, we discover in Chrétien's romances a valorization of knowing which is rational and dialectical, rather than volontaristic and mystical, and which reflects an intrusion of dialectics upon *grammatica* and rhetoric.[2] With dialectics came a more refined epistemological awareness of the difference between *things, perceptions* of things produced by the senses, and *notions* of things produced by the rational power of the intellect. Abelard writes thus:

> The soul has different natures (*vires*), corresponding to its different powers. It is animating, feeling, and thinking. The animating power, i.e. that it can animate the body and further its growth it has in common with the souls of plants and animals. The sensation it has in common only with the souls of animals. The sensation is a power of the soul exercised only by organs of the body, e.g. feeling by touch, common to all animal souls, with the hand or other parts of the body, or seeing with the eyes, and the other senses through other parts of the body as if through windows. Where there is sensation, but not yet reason, there may be imagination, but no notion because the notion is quasi the effect of reason. Reason is the power of discernment, i.e. of considering and deliberating something as existing in its specific nature (*quasi in aliqua natura vel proprietate consistens*) when someone considers a thing as a thing or as a substance, which is corporeal or sensible or coloured, or imagines (*excogitare*) it in its specific nature even if it does not exist, like the goatstag or the morrow or the laughing stone.[3]

Abelard is vehement, moreover, in denying that the forms of things that we imagine have existence or that likenesses produced by the soul are identical to the soul itself:

> If anybody asks whethere these imaginary forms, through which we have imagination or notion, are something, we say no. They are neither substances nor forms supported by substances: If, after I have seen a tower, I remember it when it is not present or completely destroyed, that immense, high, and quadrangular likeness which my mind shapes, which takes form, so to speak, before the mind's eye, is no substance and no form. . . . But someone will say . . . the intellect itself is that likeness. But we do not accept this. The intellect,

which is the form of the indivisible soul, cannot go beyond its object so as to accomodate itself to the extent of all things or to transfigure itself into all forms, nor can the soul. Therefore we maintain that these images and likenesses of things which the mind creates for itself so that it can contemplate the absent things, are nothing. (pp. 239–240)

Although grammar and dialectics had already begun to overlap by the middle of the eleventh century, the early twelfth century was a period of massive infiltration of logic into grammar. For Hugh of St. Victor, the discipline of grammar is a subcategory of logic, though he concedes that this classification is open to question:

Logic is separated into grammar and the theory of argument (*rationem disserendi*). The Greek word *gramma* means letter, and from it grammar takes its name as the science of letters . . . There are those who say that grammar is not a part of philosophy, but, so to say, an appendage and an instrument in the service of philosophy, just as the foot, hand, tongue, eyes, etc., are at once the body's parts and its instruments. Grammar, simply taken, treats of words, with their origin, formation, combination, inflection, pronunciation, and all things else pertaining directly to utterance (*pronuntiationem*) alone. The theory of argument is concerned with the conceptual content of words (*de vocibus secundum intellectus*). (*Didascalicon* 2.28, pp. 79–80)

Here is how J. Isaac describes the interaction between the disciplines in the first half of the twelfth century:

Depuis le milieu du XIIe siècle de nombreux écrits d'Aristote jusque-là inconnus ou tout au moins laissés à l'abandon, sont mis en circulation; l'enseignement sur texte de la dialectique s'en trouve considérablement élargi et les artiens voient s'ouvrir de nouveaux domaines leurs investigations. Dans ces conditions, dès que l'on possède avec la grammaire les bases indispensables, on se lance à corps perdu dans la logique et la philosophie en passant par-dessus la rhétorique, et l'on est de moins en moins attiré par les disciplines du *quadrivium*; tout naturellement aussi les *Catégories* et le *Peri hermeneias* perdent la valeur qu'ils tenaient de leur exclusivité et l'on cesse de recourir avec autant d'avidité aux commentaires de Boèce sur ces deux ouvrages.[4]

Since the mid-twelfth century, numerous of Aristotle's writings that had been either unknown or ignored began to circulate. The teaching of dialectics on the basis of a text became considerably more prevalent, and the the practitioners of the art found their investigations extended to new domains. In such circumstances, as soon as one acquired the indispensible basics of grammar, one threw oneself wholeheartedly into logic and philosophy, bypassing rhetoric. The attractions of the quadrivium diminished more and more. Quite naturally, the *Categories* and the *Peri hermeneias* lost the value that they had because of their exclusivity, and one turned less avidly to Boethius's commentary on these two works.

According to R. W. Hunt, who has studied twelfth-century glosses on Priscian, "This preoccupation with questions of logic is the distinguishing mark of the early twelfth-century glossators. They were not engaged in teaching the rudiments. They were addressing students who had mastered the elements and who had made some progress in dialectic."[5] Hunt accounts for the confluence of disciplines as follows:

> Such an encroachment is easily understood, when we consider that their two main sources, Priscian and Boethius, stimulated inquiry into the logic of language, and that dialectical questions have never aroused more passionate interest than at the time when these glosses were written. Furthermore, the terminology of the two branches of study was largely the same. Priscian uses the words substance and quality in his definition of the noun, and speaks of the accidents of the various parts of speech. It is not surprising that the early glossators were unsuccessful in separating the grammatical and logical uses of such terms, though they tried hard to do so. (pp. 22–23)

During this early period of convergence of grammar and logic, the use of literary illustrative quotations waned, and the purpose of *grammatica* ceased to be primarily the study and imitation of the classical authors, even though the same masters taught both exercises. Roughly at the same time that the *Roland* was probably transcribed, a new concern arose among grammarians to understand how the meanings of words determined each other in our utterances, that is, to study the syntactic dimension of semantics. As G. L. Bursill-Hall puts it:

> The generation of grammarians following Peter Helias achieved a synthesis between logic in grammar and the study of classical authors; such a synthesis was achieved in the study of syntax, and it is from this time that the first independent treatises on syntax date. As early as the second half of the 12th century we find separate treatises on syntax and this became the outlet for the grammarian's interest in logical analysis. In this respect the work of Ralph of Beauvais is significant, since it is in his work that the development of syntactic theory and the renewal of the study of classical authors appears.[6]

At the same time, an interesting shift occurred in grammatical doctrine concerning the epistemic function of verbal signs: language came to be seen by the grammarian as an instrument, not of human will but of reason. Hunt observes that

Petrus Helias had said that the general cause of the invention of words was that men might have a means of showing their will (*uoluntas*) to one another. In the gloss *Tria sunt* this becomes "that we might have a means of expressing our concepts (*intellectus*) and of showing them to others." The significant change is the substitution of *intellectus* for *uoluntas*, and the point of it is made plain by a passage in the gloss *Promissimus*. The glossator says that in all conversation, that is in the speech of one man to another, three things are necessary, a thing supponed, a concept and a word—a thing so that there may be discourse concerning it, a concept so that by it we may know the thing and a word so that by it we may represent the concept. (pp. 32-33)

Such epistemological distinctions, now so easily made by grammarians, had been impossible in the *Roland*, and that impossibility was a determining element of the tragedy of that poem. Had Roland been less willfull and more reasonable, his *Chanson* would never have existed. Hunt continues by claiming that with Petrus Helias and with Ralph of Beauvais (who had come as a student from England to France by 1140), the boundaries between grammar and logic were once again distinct, even though a logical intelligence persisted in the systematic exploration of syntax. *Grammatica* once again became responsive to poetry, and new poetic examples began to be drawn by grammarians from the classical poets and freely used along with the old. Surely the active recourse to Ovid by twelfth-century grammarians contributed the new concern with structure and form in courtly Ovidianism. According to Hunt, Ralph of Beauvais was widely known as a man learned in profane as well as sacred letters and was still teaching grammar in the 1180s (p. 50), hence, while Chrétien was in his prime.

By the second half of the twelfth century, the logical corpus was abundant and included translations of the whole of Aristotle's *Organon*, all of Cicero's and Boethius's extant logical commentaries and writings, and also a properly medieval tradition of logical thought embodied in works by Augustine, Alcuin, John Scot Eriugena, Garlandus Compotista, Anselm, and Abelard. Thus, Chrétien belonged to a culture whose intellectuals could confidently meet the classical logicians on their own terrain. It is surely no coincidence that on their side, vernacular poets could now presume to welcome into their young language the great poetic legends of classical antiquity as well—those of Thebes, Troy, Alexandria, and Rome.[7]

Abelard describes the logician's venture thus:

In writing a logical treatise, this order must be followed: since arguments are composed from a sequence of propositions, and since propositions are formed from words, he who writes thoroughly about logic must begin with simple terms, then write about propositions, and then complete his logic with arguments, according to the example of our master Aristotle, who devoted his *Categories* to terms, his *Peri her-*

meneias to propositions, and his *Topics* and *Analytica* to arguments.[8]

Surely the prospect of systematically combining words into propositions, and of disposing propositions as valid arguments whose truth could pertain *to* reality, yet be ontologically distinct *from* reality, was invaluable to a burgeoning poetics of written vernacular fiction. For fiction, too, was a discourse whose textual utterances could presume to reflect things that truly exist, yet whose truth could be autonomous from what exists because such truth resided in the internal coherence of the story itself.

When theories of the proposition diverge from the grammarian's conception of the sentence as a mere "competent conjunction" (*competens conjunctio*) of words or as a "complete construction" (*constructio perfecta*), logic begins to offer concepts and examples fecund to poets as "makers," not of arguments, but of vernacular stories.[9] If *grammatica* may be considered as the art of marshalling signs into sentences whose rightness does not depend on referring rightly, logic may be seen as the art of marshalling sentences into a discourse whose truth does not depend on what "is," but upon their *consignifying* coherently: both grammar and logic deal with language that is empty. Following Aristotle and Boethius, Abelard held that a proposition is composed minimally of a noun and a verb, and that the verb makes an assertion ("Socrates runs"). The two terms forming a proposition correspond to an intellection, and they signify that intellection before they signify things. As a combination of a noun and a verb, a proposition is a predicative act whose object may be a single being, but one thought about from different points of view and expressed by different terms. The meaning of a proposition is therefore not reducible to its separate terms, but signifies as a whole. A proposition's truth is neither wholly in the intellect nor wholly in the thing intellected, but in between. Thus, a proposition expresses a "something" that is not an existing thing (*essentia*), but a "sort of thing" (*quasi res*), a "nothing at all" (*nihil omnino*), an "absolutely nothing" (*nullam omnino rem*) (Jolivet, pp. 81–82). Because it does not exist, but is outside of being, the meaning of a proposition escapes from the limits of material being; but what it loses on the plane of ontology, it gains on the plane of logic. Hence, the formal truth, but ontological error, of the statement that if all men are birds and Socrates is a man, Socrates is a bird. The whole mechanism of dialectical consequences develops in a domain exterior to things and even to ideas (Jolivet, p. 84).

An argument is a discursive unit comprised of a sequence of propositions, and, as Abelard defines it, is "something inducted rationally by dialectical reasoning which brings faith to something doubtful, that is, to a proposition about which there was doubt" (Jolivet, p. 138). A syllogism, for Abelard, is a complete and perfect inference. An argument, however, is distinct from argumentation: a physicist, Abelard says, makes arguments, but he learns the discipline of argumentation from the philosopher (*Logica ingredientbus*, p. 2).

If an argument is a sequence of propositions, so too, a kernel story is a discrete discursive unit made up of a sequence of narrative statements or events. Like a proposition, a narrative event is composed minimally of a noun and a verb, with the verb predicating some perceived state or happening in time, some "accident," and the truth of a series of consignificant, fictive events is inherent to narrative discourse itself, and not to reality. An event expresses a relationship between things that has been perceived or postulated by the mind of the narrator. Both a proposition and a narrative statement reflect "happenings" which are above all mental phenomena, in the root sense of that term (*phanaein* means "to shine," "to appear"), in that they express "phantasies" or presentations of reality to the mind. (The Aristotelian term for "proposition" was *logos apophantikos* or *apophansis*.)[10] It is worth noting that the impact of logic was accompanied by a willingness, on the part of William of Conches, to redefine *fabula* not as the realm of unbridled fantasy (as Cicero did, *De inventione* 1.19.27), but rather as "whatever has been or can be construed in fiction" (*omne illud quod confingitur vel confingi potest*). Furthermore, William also gave maximal breadth to the notion of *argumentum*, which he stated to mean "rational argument by which doubtful things are proved," "fictive things which cannot occur," "brief summaries of material," or else "metaphorical discourse" (*quod nos similitudo aliqua arquit*) (*Glossae Super Macrobius*, p. 69).

The fiction of romance is a sequence of *avantures* or "happenings" (or else, "accidents," in the logical sense of that term). If an "event" (Old French, *avenement*) demands a complete narrative "proposition" of subject plus verb, Chrétien's narrative propositions engage criteria of credibility or probability that exploit (or contest) criteria of necessity proper to modal logic as well. The narrator himself often questions or defends such necessity in his story, and Chrétien's characters often exercise their judgment and act according to logical necessity (or, just as importantly, conspicuously in *defiance* of it). Furthermore, what happens in Chrétien's stories happens as much *in* his heroes as *to* them or *by* them, which is to say that Chrétien often fictionalizes, through his heroes, dilemmas of perception and judgment that were also matters of concern to the logicians of his time.[11] There is, in short, a strongly hermeneutical dimension to Chrétien's notion of *avanture*, and this dimension is only reinforced whenever Chrétien transgresses or parodies laws of logical reasoning. In a recent book, Daniel Poirion has described the different types of "marvelous" (*le merveilleux*) that characterize the major vernacular genres of medieval literature, among them, the marvelous of twelfth-century epic and romance.[12] While in the *Roland*, the marvelous corresponds to "an esthetics of force" (p. 20), the marvelous of romance is linked with the quest for *sens* or *senefiance* and even with the very process of *écriture*, understood as a pleasure in subtlety. (What Poirion calls *écri-*

ture, I am calling *grammatica*.) Speaking of Marie de France, Poirion says (pp. 64-65) that

> l'auteur des *Lais* fait allusion à ces gloses des modernes qui rendent aux texte "de leur *sen* le surplus" (Prologue, v. 16), et à l'intelligence des nouveaux écrivains "plus . . . subtils de sens" (v. 20). Nous avons là un système complexe: conte breton + *sen* de la glose + *sens* de l'écriture. Mais pour bien le comprendre il faut le compléter parce qu'il y a avant et après. Avant, dans un passé confus, le mythe archaïque dont le conte, puis le récit romanes que gardent le souvenir fragmentaire. Après, on a cet effet de lecture à quoi l'on attribue la plaisance, et que nous pouvons rattacher au problème du merveilleux. (pp. 64-65)

> The author of the *Lais* alludes to these glosses of the moderns which give to the texts "the surplus of their meaning" (Prologue, l. 16), to the minds of new writers "more subtle meanings" (l. 20). We have here a complex system: Breton tale + meaning of the gloss + meaning of the text. But in order to understand it well, it must be completed by what came before and after. Before, there was a confused past, an archaic myth that the tale, and then the romance narrative, preserve as a fragmented memory. After, there comes the effect of reading associated with pleasure and with the problem of the marvelous.

Poirion suggests, however cautiously, that the *senefiance* of the marvelous, which is linked to the pleasure of the text, also rejoins the deep, hidden substance of the archaic myth. While I am in agreement with, and shall later extend, Poirion's intuition, for now, I would add quite simply that the "marvelous" subtlety of early romance *écriture* constitutes itself specifically as a transgression of the subtlety of logical reasoning, *while exploiting it at the same time*. I would add, furthermore, that a similar tension marks the *Tristan* material as well: in one instance, Iseut both lies by *intention* and tells the truth *in fact* when she claims in her trial that no man but her husband and the leper who has carried her across the stream on his shoulders (Tristan in disguise) were ever between her thighs; and in a second instance, Iseut reasons logically about the identity of the fool in Mark's court (again, Tristan in disguise). Moreover, Matilda T. Bruckner has recently underscored the play of truth as fiction in the *Tristan d'Oxford* as a reflection of that poem's status as a vernacular text.[13] Like the *Tristan* poets, Chrétien seems concerned to assign epistemological limits to the claims of logical truth in his fiction, that is, to show us that fiction can perfectly well *include* logical necessities without being *constrained* by them. In short, if Chrétien was exposed, in his training as a young *clerc*, to the "logical" grammar of his age, now a more worldly Chrétien seems to want to reclaim, as the grammarians were themselves beginning to do, the rights of poetic understanding, and it is within this dialectic of cultural imperatives that Chrétien invents and deploys his new marvelous.[14]

Although Chrétien himself never makes known his thoughts about the relationship between narrative fiction and logic, within fifty years of his supposed period of composition, a relationship between logical hermeneutics and modes of narrative "truth" did become an active issue with the grammarian and rhetorician John of Garland. Writing, probably between 1231 and 1235, John mentions in his *Parisiana poetria* a broad category of "interpretive" narrative that is called "hermeneutic" (*ermeneticon*). This includes all narrative that is alien to legal causes and is of two basic types: "One is rooted in plot, the other in character." The kind rooted in plot or structure has three species or parts, namely, *fabula*, *historia*, and *argumentum*. A "fable," John says, "contains events that are untrue, and do not pretend to be true; it follows that avoiding vice in fabulous narrative means lying with probability, as it says in the *Art of Poetry*." "A history," John continues, "reports an event which has taken place long before the memory of our age." The third term, *argumentum*, is more elusive. I am not satisfied, for example, by the term "realistic fiction" which is Traugott Lawler's way of translating it, for it insists too much on a notion of narrative truth as an effect of the mimetic. The definition of *argumentum*, though it certainly implies a sense of the probable, seems to suggest that a plot is probable when it is architectonically or formally coherent, that is, structured, just as an argument must be logically structured in order to be (probably) correct or true. *Argumentum*, according to John, is something constructed (*res ficta*), "which nevertheless could have happened, as in the case of comedies. And no invocation should be made in a comedy, except for an insoluble complication in the plot . . . That is, a god shold not be called on unless an insoluble complication develops."[15]

Chrétien's much discussed term *conjointure* expresses, then, a syntagmatic notion of truth lacking in traditional epic, a sense that, like terms in a proposition, things and events not only signify, but *con*signify, which is to say that their significations become mutually determining in narrative discourse. Many critics have sought the implications of *conjointure* in classical and medieval treatises on rhetoric and poetics in order to account for Chrétien's virtuosity as an architect of narrative form. However, the classical writers are not very illuminating on this subject. Quintilian, for example, considers "conjoined discourse" (*sermo coniunctus*) as *stylistic* continuity or else as the systematic exploitation of figures of thought (*translatio*),(*Institutio oratoria* 8.3.40). Critics have not had any better results with twelfth-century rhetorical treatises. Douglas Kelly writes that "the treatment of invention and disposition seemed to most critics completely inadequate; here the authors had very little to say of real significance. That they say little is certainly true; and, as the same scholars found in studying the arts of poetry, their instruction is not very inspired or inspiring."[16] Although Chrétien underwent enormous influence of rhetorical theory in the area of tropes and figures, as Peter Haidu and others have shown, I suggest that his poetic technique in *Yvain* was so innnovative in questions of structure and form because his most fecund models came more from logic than from rhetoric.[17] John of Garland, writing after Chrétien, was less of a theoretician on this score, then, than an observer of literary *faits accomplis*. In short, if twelfth century rhetoric is strong in dealing with all of those figural resources of speech that exploit and amplify the inherent equivocity of conventional signs, the goals of twelfth-century logic are quite opposite: logic teaches us how to overcome the radical equivocity of conventional signs and to utter truths that are univocal, distinct, necessary, and permanent. One science of discourse is centrifugal, playful, relativistic, opportunistic, and subversive; the other is centripetal, serious, totalizing, constant, and recuperative. Both forces exert themselves wholly within the order of discourse itself, at the expense of the myth of referentiality, and the tension between them is an important constituent of twelfth-century vernacular poetics.

Chrétien's interest in the actual process of dialectical reasoning is evident already in *Erec et Enide*, for at one point in that romance such reasoning enters into the dramatic action of his characters. When Erec defeats Yder, the knight who had insulted Guenevere at the beginning of the romance, Erec orders his captive to precede him back to Arthur's court as a sign announcing that a victory has occurred. Guenevere and Gawain watch Yder's approach from a window, and the window accentuates the opposition between inner and outer, between objects perceived and the understanding of objects – an opposition that Abelard also metaphorized as a "window," as we saw before. When existing things are perceived, they become signs, and such signs become equivocal when they enter the intellect, as do *words* as signs. Chrétien interrupts the trajectory of his story in order to highlight the interpretation of Yder's equivocal approach: has Erec venged Guenevere by defeating Yder? or has Yder defeated Erec? Erec has deliberately created what we may call a hermeneutical situation, one where interpretation becomes heroic action in its own right. Formally speaking, the question that Guenevere and Gawain ponder is what Abelard called a *questio quaerens*, that is, an interrogative proposition that is really composed of two contradictory propositions where there is doubt as to which one is true (Jolivet, p. 192). This is an exercise in probable argumentation, as opposed to the demonstrative or sophistical:

> Lors s'est la reïne esmeüe
> as fenestres s'an est venue,
> lez mon seignor Gauvain s'estut;
> le chevalier molt bien conut:
> "Haï! fet ele ce est il.
> Molt a esté an grant peril;

conbatuz s'est. Ce ne sai gié,
se Erec a son duel vangié
ou se cist a Erec vaincu,
mes molt a cos an son escu;
ses haubers est coverz de sanc,
del roge i a plus que del blanc.
—Voïr est, fet mes sire Gauvains;
dame, je sui trestoz certains
que de rien nule ne mantez:
ses haubers est ansanglantez,
molt est hurtez et debatuz;
bien pert que il s'est conbatuz;
savoir poons, sanz nule faille,
que forz a esté la bataille.
Ja li orrons tel chose dire
don nos avrons ou joie ou ire,
ou Erec l'anvoie a vos ci
an prison an vostre merci,
ou s'il se vient par hardemant
vanter antre nos folemant
qu'il a Erec vaincu ou mort.
Ne cuit qu'autre novele aport."
Fet la reine: "Je le cuit."
—Bien puet estre", ce diënt tuit.

(ll. 1137–1165)

The the queen became stirred and came to the window and stood by
my lord Gauvain; she recognized the knight very well: "Ah!" she said,
"it's he! He has been through great danger; he has fought. I do not
know whether Erec has avenged his grievance or whether this man has
vanquished Erec, but his shield has taken many blows; his hauberk is
covered with blood. There is more red on it than white." "True," said
my lord Gauvain; "lady, I am very certain that you are in no way lying: his hauberk is bloody, very dented and beaten in. It is very obvious that he has fought, and we may infer without the least error that
the battle was hard. Surely what we will hear will bring joy or grief:
either Erec sends him here to you to be the prisoner of your mercy, or
else he comes in arrogance to boast foolishly amongst us that he has
defeated Erec to the death. I do not believe there can be any other
outcome." The queen said, "I believe it." "It may well be," they all
said.

Although this hermeneutical episode staged by Erec and decoded by Guenevere and Gawain is not indispensable to Chrétien's plot, and although the answer
to their *quaestio* comes not in the form of inferences drawn by them, but from
the logic of the story itself, such speculations by characters about events as they
unfold in the story of their world call attention to the kind of cognitive efforts
that Chrétien demands of his own audience. If we compare this moment to that
in the *Roland* where Charlemagne and the Franks hear and interpret Roland's
horn, we see that a considerable shift has occurred in modalities of heroic consciousness: for Charlemagne, truth in external events is something intuitively
recognized; for Guenevere and Gawain, truth must be rationally deduced.

In *Yvain*, epidsodes of dialectical thinking become pivotal, by which I mean
that conclusions dialectically founded by characters both figure in and determine
the course of events that make up the plot. A much discussed case in point is
Laudine's dispute with herself as to whether she may love the knight who has
just slain her husband. The question is emotionally charged, to say the least, and
Laudine must first discipline her emotions, as Lunette bids, so as to deal with
it rationally. Psychology is momentarily subordinated to reason, as the exercise
of logic demands. During Yvain's imagined "trial," a sequence of logical operations transpire in Laudine's mind which radically alter his status in the world,
and these may be summarized as follows. If ladies love knights for their valor,
valor is not a substance, but an accident that may be in *many* substances. Therefore valor did not die with Esclados. Moreover, since accidents (unlike substances) are relative, and admit "more" or "less," if Erec beat Esclados, he is
relatively more valorous than Esclados was.[18] Since Esclados would have killed
Yvain if Esclados had won, Yvain committed no grievance when he killed Esclados. If he committed no grievance against Esclados, he certainly had no intention to commit a grievance against the person of Laudine. Thus, Laudine
"proves" to herself that she has no right to despise Yvain. Once this logical question has been resolved, the greater necessity of passionate love quickly supplants
the lesser necessity of modal reasoning, and the plot speeds on:

> Si le desresne tot einsi,
> Con s'il fust venuz devant li,
> Lors si comance a pleidoiier:
> "Va!" fet ele, "puez tu noiier
> Que par toi ne soit morz mes sire?"
> "Ce", fet il, "ne puis je desdire,
> Ainz l'otroi ben."—"Di donc, por quoi?
> Feïs le tu por mal de moi,
> Por haine ne por despit?"
> "Ja n'aie je de mort respit,
> Si onques por mal de vos le fis."

"Donc n'as tu rien vers moi mespris,
Ne vers lui n'eüs tu nul tort;
Car, s'il poïst , il t'eüst mort.
Por ce mien esciant cuit gié
Que j'ai bien et a droit jugié."
Einsi par li meïsmes prueve
Que droit, san et reison i trueve,
Qu'an lui hai."r n'a ele droit.

(ll. 1757–75)

Thus she debates, as if he were before her, and she begins to plead:
"Now," she says, can you deny that my lord was killed by you?"
"This," he says, "I cannot deny; thus, I clearly grant it." "Tell me,
then, why? Did you do it to harm me, out of despite or hatred?" "May
death never spare me if ever I did it to harm you." "Therefore, you
did nothing to harm me, nor did you wrong him, for, had he been
able, he would have killed you. It seems to me that I judged well and
rightly." Thus by herself she proves that it is right, sensible, and just
that she has no right to despise him.

Although Laudine exclaims afterward that she would like to remain in Lunette's "school," the purity and objectivity of her logic are of course questiona-
ble. At a time when logicians themselves were careful to discriminate between
logic and rhetoric, surely Chrétien was aware that Laudine is using logic rhetorically here that is, with a particular end in view.

If Chrétien keeps an ironic perspective upon logic as an instrument of pure
reason (or, by extension, of justice), he does not denounce it. Indeed, Chrétien
seems eager at times to dispose the resources specific to romance narrative in
such a way as to emulate the formal methods of dialectics. Near the end of
Yvain, two close friends, Yvain and Gawain, are unknowingly brought by the
force of circumstances into combat with each other, and Chrétien asks dialectically whether it is possible that such enemies who hate each other may still be
said to love each other as friends:

"Oïl" vos respong et "nenil."
Et l'un et l'autre proverai,
Si que reison i troverai."

(ll. 6002–4)

"Yes," I reply, and "no." And I will prove both one and the other, and
will find the argument for it."

Surely Chrétien was aware that he was raising a venerable question—that of
the possibility of contraries coexisting in a single substance—a question that was

a matter of active debate among the logicians of his time (Jolivet, p. 110). Moreover, Chrétien's boast that he will "find" the argument (*reison i troverai*) is an index of his awareness of dialectical topical theory, understood as the method for either "finding" or judging arguments. (We shall deal with topical theory and its bearing upon Chrétien's narrative shortly.) Chrétien dispels his own apparent logical contradiction by explaining that Yvain and Gawain do truly love each other, but that they are now prepared to destroy each other because they do not know that they are adversaries in battle. Their love and hatred are not contraries because they result from separate causes. Having "proved" the "marvel" that Love and Hatred are simultaneously involved in the joust between the two knights, Chrétien so relishes his own capacity to argue that he dialectically questions what he has just "proved," and at the same time initiates an analogy which allows him to reformulate his question more sharply:

> Par foi, c'est mervoille provee
> Qu'an a an un veissel trovee
> Amor et Haïne mortel.
> Deus! meïsmes an un ostel
> Comant puet estre le repeires
> A choses, qui si sont contreires?
> A un ostel, si con moi sanble,
> Ne pueent eles estre ansanble.
>
> (ll. 6021–28)

In faith, it's a proven marvel, that we have found Love and mortal Hatred in a single vessel. Lord! How can a single house lodge two things that are so contrary? It seems to me that they cannot be together in one house.

Chrétien's recourse to the analogy of the house as an "integral whole" with separate parts allows him to answer the question that he has just raised:[19] a human soul is like a building with several different rooms, he says, and while Love remains concealed in one of them, Hatred may choose to manifest itself on one of the balconies. Such rational distinctions can only seem very rudimentary to us, and Chrétien's analogy — or what logicians called *adjuncta* — is by scholastic standards a modest one; but we must see such poetic gestures as part of an important interdiscursive process which both liberated poetic narrative from the obsolete epistemological constraints of epic (at least as that genre is exemplified by the *Roland*) and opened vernacular poetic narrative up to the possibility of far more ambitious intellectual constructions, as embodied, for example, in the *Roman de la Rose* and the *Divine Comedy*.

Chapter 3
Selfhood and Substance in *Erec et Enide*

The play of oxymoron and of thematic opposition is a strong feature of Chrétien's narrative art, as it is of all courtly poetry. However, whenever Chrétien indulges conspicuously in a poetic convention, we may expect that he does so with a lucid artistic strategy in mind. Chrétien is not only a writer who experiments whenever he writes, but also one who draws his audience into the processes of invention and understanding, both through intrusions of the narrative voice into his stories and through dramatizations of the life of the mind in his fictive heroes.

In the case of oxymoron, Chrétien is clearly aware that dialectical debate is one formal strategy for expressing and yet of enclosing and mastering the provocations of the impossible in a framework of narrative whose closure arrests the anarchies of language and desire and points ultimately to a vision of harmonious presence of the universe to itself. However, I would suggest that the most important contributions of dialectics to Chrétien's technique and vision as an artist are to be found not at the verbal surface of contrary opinions dividing a single character's soul or of passionate dialogue between two characters, but rather at far more fundamental levels of *perception*, by both Chrétien *and* his characters, of a complex world of equivocal actions, things, and events.

Among the elementary preoccupations of twelfth-century logicians to become most fecund for narrative poets as well was the rational necessity of discriminating between substances and accidents. Such a distinction enabled poets such as Chrétien and Marie de France to conceive of human identity in terms quite different from those manifested earlier by the heroes of the *Chanson de Roland*.

There, heroic identity does not admit change, but may fulfill itself only by adhering to an *a priori* paradigm of the ideal self and its external obligations, as determined by kinship, friendship, custom and oath.[1] In such an ethical system, change or inconstancy is tantamount to treason. Heroic judgment in the present must remain subordinate to memory, which is the throne of truth in a duteous man's soul.

For Chrétien, by contrast, change within the self is both possible and necessary in a world which, itself, is also changing.[2] A change of heart can lead to truly heroic action.

Apparently in advance of the return of Aristotelian psychological theory to the intellectual program of the twelfth century, a renewal of philosophical speculation about the distinction between substances and accidents among logicians in the late twelfth century brought to poets, as well, a new apprehension of the problem of humans as creatures with a dynamic consciousness dwelling in a dynamic world. In his *Categories*, which was part of the Old Logic (hence, one of Aristotle's most widely read and assimilated logical treatises), Aristotle says that primary substances (individual human souls, by the way, are primary substances) may exhibit contradictory aspects, for "what is most characteristic of substance appears to be this: that, although it remains, notwithstanding, numerically one and the same, it is capable of being the recipient of contrary qualifications. Of things that are other than substance we could hardly adduce an example possessed of this characteristic . . . One and the same individual at one time is white, warm or good, at another time black, cold or bad" (p. 31).

Such a conception of substance was thoroughly elaborated upon by Abelard in his gloss on the *Categories* and also in his *Dialectica*, which, as it stands, begins with an attempt to define and describe substances and which maintains Aristotle's claim as to the capacity of substances to receive contraries (Jolivet, pp. 110–11). Some logicians (but not Abelard) held that if humans may be said to exist as individual substances, it is through their accidents (which are also individual) that subjects become individuals distinct from their genus and species: "Socrates is defined by his accidents"[3] Substances never have contraries, nor are they comparable, nor do they admit *degree* into their being. What is substantial is said *of* a subject; what is accidental is *in* a subject. A subject "changes in itself." As Aristotle says, "For whenever a substance admits of such contrary qualifications, it is by a change in itself. It is by a change in itself that a thing that was not becomes cold (having passed from one state to another) or a thing that was white becomes black or a thing that was good becomes bad."[4]

Although the *Categories* deals with the distinction between substance and accident, the real emphasis of that text is the proper knowledge of accidents. As Abelard writes, "Who can doubt whether the knowledge of accident belongs to the categories, since nine categories out of ten concern only accidents?" (*Glossae super Porphyrium*, p. 6). To *define* a thing is to deal with it as a substance; to *describe* a thing is to deal with accidents. If accidents may be said to "happen" (*accidere*; Old French, *avenir*), then Arthurian romance is an art of the accident—*avanture*—which "happens" *to* or *in* a noble primary substance, for instance, a knight who *now* fights and *now* loves. A heightened concern with those multiple accidents by which a single being may be said to inhabit the physical world marks Chrétien as a *modernus*, in the twelfth-century sense of the term: that is, someone concerned not only with truth and morality, but also with knowledge of the natural world.[5]

Questions concerning the inevitability and even the ethical *necessity* of accidental change within the individual subject are especially central to *Erec et Enide, Yvain*, and *Perceval*, though the specific terms of Chrétien's apprehension of the problem modulate from romance to romance. In *Erec et Enide*, which is the story of a young knight who gives himself first to the art of combat and then to the art of love, Chrétien implicitly raises this question: does individual, heroic honor preclude change? or is change not necessary to honor? In other words, is Erec's honor as a warrior diminished by his ardor in love? Can Erec be an ardent lover and remain a good warrior at the same time?

Such questions involve more than the nature of heroic identity in romance; they implicate the very language and form of romance narrative itself. The lexicon of courtly erotic discourse tends to constitute itself as oxymorons whose common denominator is the binary pair *joie/dolor*.[6] These two sentiments correspond to the soul's two basic passions, *concupiscentia* and *ira*, desire and wrath, which constitute men's appetitive faculties and whose proper *social* manifestations ideally take the forms of courteous love and chivalric combat.[7] Chrétien's task as a creator of narrative form is to "invent" a coherent story where antinomies of language, mind, and heroic action are fully expressed and "conjoined," rather than mutually suppressed.

Chrétien experiments artistically with these fundamental questions about human identity in several different modes in the *Erec*, and as he does so, his apprehension of the questions themselves deepens. In the first major segment of the romance, which extends from Erec's departure on the quest of revenge upon the discourteous knight to his marriage with Enide, Erec deals with the problem of accidental change largely in terms of extrinsic *social* roles.

The romance opens with Arthur's revival of the custom of the hunt of the White Stag and the giving of a kiss by the victor in the field to the most beautiful lady of the court. This social ritual deals with the basic problem of ensuring the possibility of social mobility among the nobility while maintaining order within this process of change. At a time when social classes, including both the nascent bourgeoisie and the nobility, were becoming defined less and less by their functions within the body politic and more and more by strict judicial terms, the problem of social mobility was obviously becoming a crucial one. It is interesting that Chrétien should insist precisely upon an ancient custom such as the hunt of the White Stag as a means of promulgating, rather of than stifling, social change.[8] Ancient custom, like the ancient texts of the *auctores*, is seen by Chrétien, as a resource that both binds *and* renews the social order, a paradox of twelfth-century modernity that would repeat itself even more dramatically in the Renaissance revivals of classical and Jewish antiquity.

Because Arthur is bound by feudal custom, the hunt of the White Stag must take place. But Arthur is unswerving in his commitment to that custom. Gauvain, however, is less committed to custom than Arthur and perhaps less visionary as well, and he voices strong resistance to change and a preference for the *status quo* for fear of total anarchy:

> "Sire, fet il, de ceste chace
> n'avroiz vos ja ne gré ne grace.
> Nos savomes bien tuit piece a
> quel costume li blans cers a:
> qui le blanc cerf ocirre puet
> par reison beisier li estuet
> des puceles de vostre cort
> la plus bele, a que que il tort.
> Maus an puet avenir molt granz,
> qu'ancor a il ceanz .vc.
> demeiseles de hauz paraiges,
> filles de rois, gentes et sages;
> n'i a nule qui n'ait ami
> chevalier vaillant et hardi
> dont chascuns desresnier voldroit,
> ou fust a tort ou fust a droit
> que cele qui li atalante
> est la plus bele et la plus gente."
>
> (ll. 41–58)

"Sir," he said, "you will gain neither pleasure nor thanks from this hunt. We all know the custom of the White Stag: whoever kills the White Stag must therefore kiss the most beautiful maiden of your court, no matter whom he offends. But great harm can come of this, since there are five hundred damsels here of high mark, daughters of kings, nobles, and wise men, and there is not one of them who does not have a valiant and hardy knight as her lover, and each will want to assert, rightly or wrongly, that she who attracts him is the most beautiful and the most noble."

That Arthur should acknowledge and even welcome passion as the primary motive of social change sets him ethically apart from the legacy of Virgilian epic, where passion is seen to destroy city after city in a pattern of cyclical violence. Chrétien's debt to Virgil as an artist was large, but ethically the two poets are at opposite poles, at least with regard to questions of passion and change in the human soul. If Virgil never acknowledged a standard of human behavior which included sexual passion, Ovid, on his side, could only celebrate—or even vaunt—sexual passion as a splendid but anarchic force in the cosmos.

The Chrétien of *Erec* and of *Yvain* is not, in this sense, more "Ovidian" than "Virgilian," but is rather closer to the platonism of his own time, especially that of the Chartrians Bernard Sylvester and Alain de Lille, who acknowledged sexual passion as that force by which Nature succeeds herself in the process of being as becoming.[9]

When Erec is received by an impoverished vavasor, who is Enide's father and his future father-in-law, we are invited to ponder the relationship between a man's intrinsically noble identity (or substance) and mere accidents of wealth or poverty. Erec later himself explains before the court, to which he has brought this impoverished but lovely maiden, that the vavasor's nobility is perfectly intact, even if his fortune is not:

> "D'un povre vavasor est fille:
> povretez mainz homes aville;
> ses peres est frans et cortois,
> mes d'avoir a molt petit pois."
> (ll. 1539–42)

"She is the daughter of a poor vavasor. Poverty lays low many a man; but her father is free and courteous, even though he possesses very little."

That the vavasor's daughter Enide is also of noble and potentially queenly substance is confirmed not only by the bestowal of the kiss of the White Stag upon her by Erec, but also by Guenevere's gesture of giving her a dress—not an old one, Chrétien specifies, but one that is "fresh and new" (ll. 1564–66).

But these are are only accidents of Enide's personal condition, and Chrétien is eager enough to insist upon the substantial or "natural" nobility of Enide (as opposed to its accidental manifestations) to summon Enide's parents to the attention of Arthur, who confirms Enide's pedigree: she is beautiful, he deems, but this is because of her beautiful lineage:

> —"Certes donc puis je tres bien dire
> que molt doit estre bele et ente
> la flors qui ist de si bele ante,
> et li fruiz miaudres qu'an i quiaut,
> car qui de boen ist, soëf iaut.

Bele est Enyde, et bele doit
estre, par reison et par droit,
que bele dame est molt sa mere,
biau chevalier a en son pere."

(ll. 6556–64)

"Certainly, then, may I say that the flower that has sprung from such a graft must surely be beautiful and noble, and the fruit must be the best that can be gathered, for what springs from something good will itself smell sweetly. Enide is beautiful, and must be beautiful, both by nature and by law, for her mother is a very beautiful woman, and she has, in her father, a beautiful knight."

Clearly, the opening segment of *Erec Enide* promulgates an ethos where a new ideology of change and exchange was being brought to bear upon an older (but not simple or complacent) concept of heroic honor based exclusively on traits of constancy and prowess. We may measure the difference between this new ethics and the old one by comparing the semantic range of the word *bel* in epic and romance.[10] In the *Roland* the word *bel* is extremely limited in semantic range. If we put aside its occurrences as an honorific term of address (*"bel sire"*), *bel* is almost without exception invoked to praise weapons, violent gestures, and warlike appearances. The Saracens, seeing the approach of Charlemagne's army, make the following observation:

Li emperere i fait suner ses greisles
E l'olifan, ki trestuz les eclairet.
Dient paien: "La gent Carlun est bele.
Bataille avrum e adurée e pesme." AOI.

The Emperor orders his trumpets to sound, and the olifant, which fills the air with brightness. The pagans say, "Charles's army is beautiful: We will have a battle that will be hard and painful."

Beauty in this older ethic is practically a synonym for raw force—or else, for the social status conferred by force. One exception to this generality is the allusion to Roland's fiancée Aude as a *bele damisele* (l. 3708), but such beauty has as its sole gesture of expression Aude's falling down dead when she hears the news of Roland's death at Ronceval. Such "beauty" is a mere analogue of male chivalric fanaticism. In *Erec et Enide* (as we see in the passage just quoted), feminine beauty not only exists in its own right, but has fully amplified modes of proving itself. For, if Aude heroically gives up her life for love of her dead lord, Enide by contrast, gives up only her virginity and is *renewed* by this happy, accidental change in her condition:

De l'amor qui est antr'ax deus
fu la pucele plus hardie:
de rien ne s'est acoardie,
tot sofri que qu'il li grevast,
ençois qu'ele se relevast,
ot perdu le non de pucele;
au matin fu dame novele.

(ll. 2048–54)

In the love that was between them, the maiden was the bolder of the
two. She was afraid of nothing: she suffered all, no matter what the
consequences. Thus, before she arose she had lost the name of virgin:
in the morning she was a new woman.

Moreover, the consummation of love between Erec and Enide unleashes, as
well, a flood of remunerations and gift-giving in the world around them: in an
Arthurian court surpassing those of Alexander and Caesar, *jouissance does* renew the social order and bring abundance, even to vernacular *jongleurs!* Here
is *translatio* at its very best:

Ce jor furent jugleor lié
car tuit furent a gré paié:
tot fu randu quanqu'il acrurent,
et molt bel don doné lor furent:
robes de veir et d'erminetes,
de conins et de violets,
d'escarlate, grise ou de soie;
qui vost cheval, qui volt monoie,
chascuns ot don a son voloir
si boen com il le dut avoir.

(ll. 2055–64)

That day, jongleurs rejoiced, for they were all payed to their satisfac-
tion. Everything was given that was owed, and very beautiful gifts
were given to them: robes of grey fur and of ermine and rabbit, and
of violet, scarlet, and grey colors, or of silk. Whoever deserved a
horse, whoever wished money, each had a gift as he wished, according to what he should have.

If Chrétien is an astute proponent of dynamism within the social order, his
bent for exploring the inner dynamism of the soul is equally strong. Thus, following the marriage between Erec and Enide, his story moves away from the
social sphere and more into the psychological. And, the more Chrétien explores
the life of the mind, the more he tends to exploit logical dilemmas in order to

highlight events of the soul, even though such dilemmas are expressed through carefully contrived narrative episodes, rather than logical arguments.

The question that Chrétien addresses in the middle portion of *Erec et Enide* is profound: can love between two individuals subsist when accidental changes of behavior occur which cannot, themselves, be loved? After his marriage with Enide, Erec becomes overindulgent in love, at the expense of his chivalry, and Enide reports to him the malevolent rumors about him that are circulating among the *médisants* of the court. Erec wrongly doubts Enide's love for him, and in order to test her loyalty he forces her to accompany him on a quest during which he commands her to remain silent, *no matter what should occur*. Each time that Erec is about to be attacked by an enemy unseen except by her, Enide must decide whether or not to speak out—and speak out she does.

Assuming that most readers will grasp a basic "rightness" in Enide's behavior, such a judgment on our part (as on hers) involves two implicit logical operations. First, we are invited to discriminate between human identity as individual substance and accidents which occur *in* or *to* that substance. Erec himself, of course, cannot yet make such a discrimination, so he assumes that the disloyal feelings among his knights that Enide reports to him are signs of her own disloyalty—hence, signs of a radical change in her nature. Out of Erec's cognitive inadequacy a good story is born. We, of course, know that Erec is mistaken in his judgment of Enide and that his own behavior toward her is an accident to be deplored, all the more since Enide's womanly obedience to Erec's command would both harm him and help his enemies. By disobeying Erec's unjust command, Enide is not being disloyal to Erec as an individual subject, but is only disregarding an improper accident that has beset that subject.

Secondly, we must see that Enide needs to solve the problem of identifying and understanding true contraries before she can act responsibly. Aristotle deals systematically with this logical problem in his *Peri hermeneias* and his *Topics*, Cicero touches on it in his own *Topica* 11.47, and Abelard elaborates upon it in his commentary on the first Aristotelean text. When contrary attributes bear upon two different subjects, we are told, these attributes do not necessarily retain their relationship of contrariety. In *Topics*, 2.7, Aristotle discusses the problem of properly construing contraries when contrary accidents bear upon two subjects, and Aristotle specifically discusses relationships between the pairs friend/enemy and help/harm: to harm a friend is clearly the contrary of helping a friend, but to harm an enemy is not the contrary of helping a friend. In short, for Enide to be disloyal to Erec's command of silence is quite proper on two scores: first, as I have said, her disloyalty is not to him as subject, but only to his accidental disposition; second, if she were to remain silent, she would not help him, rather she would help his enemy. *Helping an enemy is the true contrary of helping a friend*, so Enide's love quite rightly dictates that she *help* Erec by speaking instead of *harming* him by remaining silent.

Such distinctions were of course beyond Roland at Ronceval, when, out of loyalty to Charlemagne (and against Oliver's more logical advice), he blindly obeyed Charlemagne's command to defend the rearguard and refused to summon help. When the complexities of logical thought began to infiltrate literature, the path to true honor suddenly involved a new necessity for heroes to make decisions based on the proper exercise of judgment. It would be silly to claim that Chrétien needed to be thoroughly Aristotelean (obviously, he was not) in order to be attracted to the complexities of human reason, any more than a modern writer must be a devout Freudian systematically to explore a hero's unconscious, but it would be equally silly to deny that Aristotle (through Abelard) and Freud, each in a different epoch, radically altered the priorities of human perception as expressed in literature.[11]

If Enide (and the reader) must learn to discriminate between true loyalty to a person and loyalty which is only apparent because it is determined by changeable accidents of a person's extrinsic being rather than by that person's substance, Erec too must learn a similar lesson, even though, because of difference of sex, the two protagonists of *Erec et Enide* have different roles and espouse different modes of action. As a knight, Erec must dispel by deeds of martial prowess the doubts that have arisen in the court about the state of his chivalry, as well as doubt that has arisen in his own mind about his wife's loyalty; Enide, whose "victory" on her wedding night was achieved in a skirmish of a less martial sort, must prove her steadfastness in love by warring against temptations of adultery and of wealth, in particular, against the sexual and social aggressions of the Count Oringle de Limors. The Count chances upon Enide and her seemingly dead husband in the forest and, captivated by her beauty, spontaneously offers her the privileges of high estate if she will marry him. Enide spontaneously refuses. Pressing to win her favor, Oringle promises an honorable burial for Erec and brings the couple to his domain in Limors. He summons his chaplain and commands him to marry them, without Enide's consent: "*si li ont a force donée, / car ele molt le refusa*" ("they gave her to him by force, for she fully refused him," ll. 4732–33). When Enide rejects the Count's renewed promises of high estate in exchange for her resignation to her imposed role of spouse, the Count beats her before the assembly of his knights, who are both appalled by his brutality and sympathetic to her loyalty to Erec even in widowhood. The Count, however, claims her as his property and proclaims himself as her master: " '*la dame est moie et je sui suens, / si ferai de li mon pleisir*' " (" 'The lady is mine and I am hers; thus I will do with her what I please,' " ll. 4800–4801). Precisely when Enide vows defiance of the Count to the very death, Erec miraculously revives from his faint and slays the Count, whereupon the couple is joyously reunited. Chrétien is the first vernacular narrator to use simultaneity—temporal conjuncture—as a sign of logical *conjointure*.

As is so often the case in Chrétien's art, this episode very deftly addresses a major social issue of his age, namely the apprehension of marriage as a relationship that is at once personal, social, and divinely instituted. And the renewed science of the theologians (especially Richard of St. Victor) instigated and sharpened the new values that Chrétien so clearly endorses.[12] Not only did marriage become a sacrament during Chrétien's century, but the very notion of marriage became centered upon the exercise of free consent between legitimate partners (rather, for instance, than upon cohabitation or consummation) in a relationship that is only *afterwards* solemnized by God: *consensus facit nuptias*. Such a concept (which still endures) clearly reflects a logical distinction between marital union of two beings as a *substantially* personal one and marital union of two beings on the basis of what were seen during the twelfth century as the extrinsic or *accidental* social considerations dictated by the older customs of Germanic feudalism, where power over a woman (*nundium*) was purchased by a negotiated contract (*Verlobung*). Chrétien is meticulous about presenting the Count's point of view fairly in order that a facile judgment of the older code will not be made. It is the Count's extremism and his brutality which finally reveal the tyrannous consequences of an ethical position about marriage which at first had revealed itself in Chretien's story as plausible. This episode illustrates the extent to which the seemingly abstract techniques of logic became decisive in social and political controversies of a more concrete sort, and I may add that Chrétien's formation as a literate court poet in the administration of Henri and Marie de Champagne clearly conditioned him as a progressive interpreter of social and judicial controversies in his age.

However much Chrétien's sensitivity to social issues was sharpened by an introduction to at least basic principles of logical reasoning, we see in the Joy of the Court episode that follows the reconcilation of Erec and Enide how capable Chrétien is of deepening a question (at the same time as he extends its consequences) through the devices not of logical argumentation, but of narrative disposition. Chrétien tells the episode in such a way that we are compelled to share Erec's astonishment at an event that has "truly" occurred — even in fiction, what "happens" must be seen as truly happening — but which seems logically impossible both to Erec and to us: when Maboagrain is defeated in combat by Erec, why in the world does he rejoice? How can a knight meet his defeat in combat as if it were a victory?

Maboagrain explains why, in this case, such narrative propositions are not, in fact, contraries. He explains to Erec that as a child he had fallen in love with the lady who is now his wife. Maboagrain had unwisely sworn an oath that he would never leave the marvelous orchard in which they lived together until another knight defeated him in combat, and his lady had unwisely held him to that oath: " 'Thus my lady thought she could hold me here for a very long time,' " (" *'Einsi me cuida retenir / ma dameisele a lonc sejor'* " ll. 6040-41). This garden of seemingly paradisial beauty had thenceforth become, for him, a "prison"

(l. 6047). Because of his enduring love for his lady, Maboagrain could never bring himself to break his oath; nor, because of his inviolable sense of chivalric honor, could Maboagrain ever fight without doing his very best. For Maboagrain to be defeated now by a knight better than he is not a dishonor, for it is just; in this case it is even a victory because a bad oath has been fulfilled, but not broken. Both Maboagrain's knightly honor and his love are intact, now that this unfortunate accident of his youth has been reversed. Therefore, Maboagrain's defeat is in fact a victory over an accidental shame of his past, but not over his soul as an honorable substance.

However, the main surprise of the Joy of the Court is that Maboagrain's childhood had been spent in the court of Erec's father; moreover, Enide and his lady are first cousins: close bonds of common origin and of kinship suggest not only that the members of the two couples have shared identities (substances), but also that their relationships as married couples have even more in common. Indeed, in each couple, a knight has, by his own consent, allowed himself to be improperly circumscribed by a woman's love, owing to an improper perception of married love as a *static* human relationship, rather than as a *dynamic* one built upon the renewed freedom of choice. We may suggest, here, that Chrétien is extending a burgeoning judicial concept of marriage into a new, *non*judicial ideal of ongoing marital love based not upon constraint, but upon continually renewed freedom of choice. It is difficult for us to just know how Chrétien came to hold such opinions, whether by listening to arguments of logicians or simply by looking at the world around him with new vision: whatever the case, we may suspect that Chrétien is not only sharing in, but also helping to forge, the most radically innovative doctrines of his age.

Erec's victory over Maboagrain reinforces his victory over an undesirable aspect of himself, and it also leads to our grasp of a human problem as one that reaches beyond Erec's individual relationship with Enide to love relationships within the human species as a whole. The dilation of their consciousness of a new human truth coincides, moreover, with the reintegration of Erec and Enide into the social group, and this leads ultimately to Erec's and Enide's coronations as king and queen. Progress beyond individual selfawareness may make Erec and Enide poor candidates as forerunners of the full-blown romantic subjective hero, yet such progress does coincide with the epistemological objectives of twelfth-century logic. Although logicians did ascribe ontological priority to the individual over species and genus, the thrust of their discipline still remained that of perfecting those laws of understanding and predication according to which individuals may be said to belong to larger groups. In other words, logic in the twelfth century was a science of abstraction whose purpose, as Abelard saw it, was to permit the intellect both to transcend and to extend its perceptions of individual things. When we perceive an object through the senses, we form an image of that object. The image then becomes subject to intellection which, if correct, allows us to infer both how that image is similar to images of other individuals and how it different. This process of abstraction leads finally to intellections of universals (Jolivet, pp. 370–71).

Moreover, the closing episodes of *Erec et Enide* illustrate a movement corresponding roughly to these levels of cognition that Winthrop Wetherbee calls the "stress on transcendence."[13] Having recognized the difficult truth of their own relationship, Erec and Enide pass to an objectivization of that same truth in another couple's relationship. Progress, through abstraction, toward the discovery of universals leads to an intellectual victory that coincides very precisely with Erec's and Enide's victory as they reach, with their coronation, the top of the social order. Erec's robe during this investiture is embroidered, we are told, with the works of four fairies *"par grant san et par grant mestrie"* ("with great intelligence and great mastery," l. 6683), and these are portraits of the four sciences of the *quadrivium* by which humanity may come to true understanding of the whole of the physical universe. This quadrivial robe encloses Erec's body. His scepter, by contrast, is an object of active contemplation by the mind. Fashioned of a substance more transparent than glass, this scepter bears etched upon it the forms of every animal species existing in the creation. This is more than mere *scientia*, it is *sapientia*, and even Arthur marvels at this exalted vision of the animate world in its totality. Here the Arthurian marvelous has become the marvel of the human intellect experiencing, at a moment of fulfillment of human love and of human freedom and justice, its fullest powers of abstract knowledge. That abstract knowledge is also spiritual knowledge mediated (if Reto Bezzola is correct)[14] through the green emerald of faith:

> Li rois Artus aporter fist
> un ceptre qui molt fu loëz;
> del ceptre la façon oëz
> qui fu plus clers c'une verrine,
> toz d'une esmeraude anterine,
> et si avoit plain poing de gros.
> La verité dire vos os
> qu'an tot le monde n'a meniere
> de poisson, ne de beste fiere,
> ne d'ome, ne d'oisel volage,
> que chascuns lonc sa propre ymage
> n'i fust ovrez et antailliez.
> Li ceptres fu au roi bailliez
> qui a mervoilles l'esgarda,
> si le mist, que plus ne tarda,
> li rois Erec an sa main destre:
> or fu rois si com il dut estre;

puis ont Enyde coronee.

(ll. 6808–25)

King Arthur summoned forth a scepter which drew great praise. Hear how the scepter was fashioned. It was clearer than glass and made of a single emerald, and was as big as a fist. I shall dare to tell the truth: there was no manner of fish, of wild beast, of human, of flying bird in the world whose image was not worked there and engraved. The scepter was brought to the king, who looked upon it with marvel, and did not wait to place it in Erec's right hand: now he was a king, as he should have been; and then they crowned Enide.

This is surely one of the highpoints of what has often been called twelfth-century humanism, and it is also a moment of precocious harmony between fundamentally distinct trends in Western culture, Aristotelian rationalism and neoplatonic mysticism. As we shall see in the next chapter, Chrétien's poetics in *Yvain* took a direction that carried him away from concerns with reconciling the mystical and the rational, the transcendant and the immanent. Rather, his concern is to deploy the resources of rational thought in the service of ethics of a very social sort.

Chapter 4
Topos and Tale

If we grant first that Chrétien presents heroes for whom proper perception and argumentation are modes of action in their own right and second that Chrétien similarly challenges his audience with narrative situations and with constructions of plot which carry what we may call a hermeneutical imperative, then much remains to be said about the closely related processes of finding or "inventing" (*inveniendi*) these arguments and of evaluating (*iudicandi*) them.

Traditionally, the art of finding and evaluating arguments belongs to the theory of topics.[1] The English word "topic" is, of course, a very diffuse way of translating the Greek *topos* or the Latin *locus*, but these original terms were already embued with ambiguity in classical culture. Such ambiguity is an inevitable consequence of the fact that topical theory was an area where all three disciplines of the medieval *trivium* converged, so that different thinkers often used the term "topic" (or its classical equivalents) at the same time, but with wholly different purposes in mind.

Topical theory remains one of the most neglected and poorly understood intellectual strands of early Western culture and merits more scrutiny, both historical and theoretical. The historical dimension of topical theory is especially important not only because its evolution is rich and interesting in its own right, but also because many historically significant documents of early Western culture have to some degree been generated or touched by methods in which topical theory was instrumental. In other words, topical theory has been a determinant of the broader cultural history to which it now belongs.

The reasons for which topical theory has been so neglected by intellectual

historians and by literary critics are unclear, but are no doubt attributable in part
to the incompatibility between topical theory itself and the cognitive paradigms
of romantic philology and of classical and medieval studies in modern times such
as I evoked them in the introduction.[2]

In classical and medieval rhetoric and dialectics, topical theory was oriented
toward the goals of discovering and recognizing universal principles of effective
or probable argumentation. It was, therefore, a highly formal and structural discipline involving either the production or the evaluation of any discourse in any
circumstances where problems of internal coherence were crucial, as in matters
of justice or philosophical debate.

Philology is a historical discipline grounded upon the systematic and di-
achronic analysis of languages, documents, legends, and myths whose purpose
is to lead backward through dim corridors of time to some specific source, intention, or moment of origin, of plenitude, or of truth. Topical theory, by contrast,
was invoked to discover truth grounded *not* upon some distant origin or intention, but rather upon formal coherence in the production of utterances. Topical
theory taught thinkers how to divest their arguments of truth based on the importance of their *input* in favor of truth that was based on universal laws of proper
inference. As Richard McKeon aptly put it, "The whole function of a place is
to get it empty so that you can put something in. But if you don't get it completely
empty, it's not a place. Nevertheless, places are the sources of the discoveries
of science."[3]

To be sure, philologists could not wholly ignore topical theory, but they re-
defined it in accordance with their own originary paradigm. Thus, the great German medievalist Ernst Robert Curtius, in his *Europäische Literatur und
lateinisches Mittelalter* (Bern and Munich: Franke, 1948), developed, just before and during the Second World War (which he called the "suicide of German
culture"), a broad notion of the *historische Topik* which was not a formal genera-
tive principle, but rather any unit of *content*—be it a cliché, commonplace, literary theme, habit of thought, archetype or pattern of feeling—which is a permanent legacy of Latinity and which recurs with modulations in different epochs
of Western culture: *Man ist Europaer, wenn man civis Romanus ist* (p. 3) ("One
is European if one is a citizen of Rome."). A repertory of "historical topics" was
thereupon construed as a source of historical continuity in Western culture, and
it is not difficult to see why Curtius's topical notions were so broadly accepted
by medievalists and nonmedievalists alike during the period of anguish following the crisis of European culture that occurred with the Second World War.
However, such notions bear little relationship to topical theory as an indigenous
strain of early Western logic.

There have been serious attempts during the last two decades, especially in
Germany and the United States, to extend some of the theoretical and practical
implications of topical theory, though still as a terrain lying somewhere between

intellectual history and hermeneutical philology. Under the general heading of *Toposforschung*, a handful of German scholars have begun to refine distinctions between different kinds of topics ("historical," rhetorical, dialectical) and to seek (mainly in Jung) a deep psychological basis for the permanence of *topoi* in Western culture. Given, however, that the medieval treatises in which topical theory develops are only now being edited and seriously examined (but rarely translated), even specialists in medieval logic stress that their understanding of the history of topical theory in postclassical and scholastic thought remains sketchy.

Fortunately, during the last few years topical theory has begun to be explored as it ought to be by Eleonore Stump, and her rigorous translation of Boethius's *De topicis differentiis*, which is accompanied by precious notes and incisive essays situating Boethius's topical theory in a broader classical tradition, is a valuable introduction both to the problem and to its history. In the discussion that follows, I shall not presume either to present the history of topical theory or to enumerate its ramifications in twelfth-century culture, but I shall suggest certain ways in which topical theory seems to have infiltrated poetic practice, specifically in demanding new criteria for coherence in narrative art. In doing so, I shall rely heavily upon Boethius's treatise (and upon Stump's scholarship), anachronous though such an undertaking might seem at first. My reasons for doing so are the following. In the twelfth century, the major classical sources of topical theory were Aristotle, Cicero, and Boethius. Although the topical treatises of all three classical writers were current in the more influential intellectual centers of France by the mid-twelfth century (for instance, all three were part of the curriculum of the School of Chartres), there was a tendency among medieval thinkers to read the earlier *auctores* through the later ones. Thus, just as Cicero had proposed to interpret Aristotle's *Topics*, so Boethius undertook to synthesize the Aristotelian tradition and the Ciceronian in his *De topicis differentiis*, and this latter Boethian treatise remained especially prominent in the twelfth- and thirteenth-century curriculum. Boethius's *De topicis differentiis* was a standard introductory textbook for the study not only of dialectics in the later ages — one that Chrétien himself would most likely have read — *but also of rhetoric* (Leff, pp. 4–6). The fourth and last book of Boethius's treatise circulated and was taught separately with the latter priority in mind, and it provided, with a brief summary of the art of rhetoric as a whole, cogent insights into the discipline of rhetoric that rhetoricians themselves had never expressed. As Boethius says, "We have received no tradition from the ancient authors on this subject, for they taught the particulars but did not work at the whole at all. Let us undertake this missing part of [their] teaching as best we can."[4]

Boethius's purpose in defining rhetoric as a discipline was to prepare himself to make careful distinctions between rhetorical and dialectical topics, distinctions that would be maintained by later logicians such as Abelard. Like Aristotle, Boethius considers both rhetoric and dialectics as disciplines that teach argumentation, and he holds, further, that both disciplines draw on topics (*topoi* or *loci*) as foundations for the arguments that they construct. Boethius wishes to make a clear distinction between two types of topic, the dialectical and the rhetorical, because he feels that such a distinction is insufficiently maintained by Cicero in his *Topica*. Cicero is mainly concerned, Boethius says (Bk. IV, p. 95), with rhetorical argumentation:

> Cicero's *Topica*, which he published for C. Trabatius, who was skilled at law, does not examine how one can dispute about things themselves but how arguments of the rhetorical discipline may be produced, which we explained more thoroughly in the commentaries we wrote on Cicero's *Topica*. How one disputes about them with dialectical arguments [*rationibus*] we explained in the commentaries we wrote on Aristotle's *Topics*, translated by us. (Bk. 4, p. 95)

Although Aristotle himself is not wholly intelligible to us in his distinctions between rhetorical and dialectical topics and although Boethius may not have resolved even for himself the ambiguities in Aristotle, we nevertheless find in the Boethian text a clearcut statement regarding the difference between rhetorical and dialectical topics, at least as *he* understood it. The rhetorical topic, he says, is rooted in arguments concerning circumstances and facts, while the dialectical topic pertains to truths whose laws are universal and eternal. However, Boethius emphasizes that even the truth of rhetorical arguments derives from laws of truth proper to dialectics:

> The differences are that the dialectical Topics are suited also for theses, but rhetorical Topics are suited for hypotheses only, that is, they are arrogated to questions informed by circumstances. For as the disciplines are distinguished from one another by the universality [of the one] and the particularity [of the other], so also their Topics differ in range and restriction, because the range of dialectical Topics is greater. Since they are independent of circumstances, which produce individual cases, they are useful not only for theses but also for arguments put forth in hypotheses, whose Topics, composed of circumstances, they included and range over.
>
> So the rhetorician always proceeds from dialectical Topics, but the dialectician can be content with his own Topics . . . Dialectic discovers arguments from qualities themselves; rhetoric from things taking on a quality. So the dialectician [discovers arguments] from genus, that is, from the nature of genus; the rhetorician from the thing that is the genus. The dialectician [discovers arguments] from similarity; the rhetorician, from a similar, that is, from the thing which takes on similarity. In the same way, the former [discovers arguments] from a contrariety; the latter, from a contrary. (Bk. 4, p. 94)

Boethius's treatise does more than to make distinctions between rhetorical and dialectical topics: it creates a hermeneutical distance from rhetoric which makes us aware that if rhetorical arguments are true, the truth of such arguments lies not in their actual performance, but in hidden laws of *argumentatio*. An argument, which only proves something, is not the same as argumentation, which is the concern for the actual *process* of proving something. As Abelard put it, in a treatise on topics of his own, "Argument is not the same as argumentation. For that which only proves [something] is an argument. We call argumentation the very constitution of proving and of proof, as in syllogism and in enthymeme taken as a whole, so we may say that argument is contained in argumentation as a part in a whole."[5] In other words, a reader of Book 4 of Boethius's *De topicis differentiis*, which Leff (p. 3) calls "the logician's rhetoric" (p. 3) or, for that matter, the reader of Abelard will suddenly become aware that the internal truth or coherence of a narrative (fictive or not) lies outside that narrative and that its basis may be apprehended as a set of laws for narrating (or arguing) properly that are divorced from any *specific* story or argument. As a metarhetoric, dialectics becomes metafiction as well, and it is this very awareness of the metafictive that sets Chrétien apart from poets who are *merely* rhetorical, though rhetorical Chrétien himself was.[6] Chrétien's art (and even the characters and the fictive narrator who inhabit that art) constantly point beyond "circumstances" (in the Boethian sense of that term) to the noncontextual reasons by which we *judge* these circumstances and apprehend their consequences. The rules according to which poets, as rhetoricians, generate stories may very well be practical, but when expressed abstractly, they are identical to the rules of dialectical argument. Such is Boethius's point in Book 4 of his *De topicis differentiis* (pp. 93-94).

Despite the lucidity of Boethius's Book 4 concerning the relationship between rhetorical and dialectical topics and despite the centrality of topical theory to twelfth-century dialectics (fully a third—over two hundred pages—of Abelard's *Dialectica* is devoted to topical theory), medieval rhetoricians themselves remained more or less within the epistemological limits that Boethius so accurately saw in their discipline. Two recent articles by Douglas Kelly attempt to define topical invention in rhetoric as illustrated by Matthieu de Vendôme and Geoffroi de Vinsauf.[7] In Matthieu, topical invention is part of *descriptio*, which (as in the Boethian elaboration of "circumstances") has two main goals, that of describing persons and that of describing action (*negotio*).[8] *Descriptio* is a process of mental clarification or elaboration (Kelly uses the French and German *éclaircissement* and *Erläuterung* as modern equivalents), and *descriptio* seems to me to correspond to the moment when, according to Abelard, confused and indistinct images of things communicated by the senses to the memory are then clarified and elaborated upon by the intellect (Jolivet, pp. 365-73). Topical invention occurs during this mental process of *descriptio*. Here, according to Kelly, is how the process is understood by the rhetorician Matthieu:

L'invention des topiques comporte trois étapes: 1. l'invention du *locus*;
2. l'invention de l'*argumentum* dans le *locus*; et 3. l'*amplificatio* de
l'*argumentum*. Elles correspondent à l'*imaginatio*, l'*excogitatio* et la
qualitas dans la composition selon Mathieu de Vendôme. D'abord on
identifie un lieu (*locus, τοπos*) dans la matière quand un éclaircissement semble à la fois souhaitable et possible. Ensuite, on décide du
contenu de cet éclaircissement d'après la conception qu'on se fait de
l'oeuvre; l'argument sert ainsi à interpréter la matière, à la rendre
vraisemblable. Enfin, l'argument est disposé dans la matière et y est
adapté selon 11 la technique de l'amplification. ("La spécialité," p. 104)

The invention of topics implies three steps: 1. the invention of the *locus*; 2. the invention of the *argumentum* in the *locus*; and 3. the *amplificatio* of the *argumentum*. These correspond to *imaginatio, excogitatio*, and *qualitas* in composition, according to Matthieu de
Vendôme. First, we identify a place (*locus, τοπos*) in the material
when a clarification becomes both desirable and possible. Then, we decide on the content of that clarification, according to the conception we
hold of the work; the argument thus serves to interpret the material
and to make it probable. Finally, the argument is deployed in the material and is adapted to it according the technique of amplification.

To the extent that it neither derives from abstract principles of cognition nor
demands their perception, Matthieu's "topography" (at least, as Kelly defines it)
remains strictly rhetorical, or circumstantial, in the sense that Boethius gives to
that term, and in no way dialectical, and therefore leads not to the production
of formal arguments (and much less to a concern with *argumentatio*), but only
to coherence and probability in unbroken narrative and description. Although
Kelly believes that the rhetorician's *descriptio* gives rise to the *beles conjointures*
of successful narrative ("Logic," pp. 12–13), I would propose that Chrétien had
come to accept dialectic as a metarhetoric and that he was himself (and wanted
his readers also to become) aware of principles for inventing and evaluating
fiction that are "topical" in a more abstract dialectical sense of that term.

To illustrate such a claim, however, calls for a discussion of topical theory
that is more detailed and concrete. Accordingly, in the pages that follow, I shall
first take a closer look at topical theory in a dialectical perspective, and then I
shall suggest that there are signs of a nonrhetorical and specifically dialectical
topography underlying the "circumstances" of Chrétien's narrative world, and I
shall suggest that logicality is even a precondition of the *merveilleux* in *Yvain*,
and perhaps in other romances as well.

In his *De topicis differentiis*, Boethius makes a distinction between two kinds
of topic, the "maximal proposition" and the *differentia* of a maximal proposition.
The former topics are self-evident propositions whose irreducible truth forms

the basis for other propositions construed as true arguments. Writing on Boethius, Eleonore Stump says:

> Boethius's maximal propositions seem to be just such self-evident truths. All true propositions, Boethius seems to be saying, are either self-evident or not self-evident; those that are not self-evident are shown to be true by being traced back to self-evident propositions. Hence, self-evident propositions provide the basis of belief for all argument. The conclusion of an argument is derived either from a maximal proposition or from propositions that are themselves derived, directly or indirectly, from maximal propositions. (p. 182)

A maximal proposition is the most basic foundation of true inferences, while *differentiae*, or "different" topics, are *species* of maximals and, as such, serve only to orient us in the process of "finding" an argument, though the argument's truth ultimately rests on the maximal.

Abelard defines maximal propositions as "those rules which, containing the sense of multiple consequences, demonstrate a common inference according to the same force (*vis*) of a relationship."[9] Abelard gives the following and absolutely classical example of a maximal: "when species is predicated of something, so too is genus" (*de quocumque species, et genus, Dialectica*. p. 310). Such a maximal proposition allows us to infer that "if it is a human, it is an animal;" or that "if it is a pearl, it is a stone;" or that "if it is a rose, it is a flower;" or that "if there is red, there is a color." In each case, a single relationship (*habitudo*) is expressed, and the truth of that relationship is independent of its content: the copula has been, so to speak, de-ontologized. Thus, all arguments "from the species" may be grouped together as the differential topic "from species."

Moreover, such arguments hold eternally (*ab aeterno*) because the maximal proposition by which we infer something is invariably true and irreducibly self-evident, even if humanity itself has not yet been created, or even if humanity has been destroyed (Jolivet, pp. 153–54). The condition of being a human being quite simply cannot "hold" (*consistere*) without the condition of being an animal (Jolivet, p. 154). As we shall see shortly, such a logical perception, as well as the specific example illustrating it ("if it is a human, it is an animal"), is radically important as a "topical" foundation for Chrétien's *Yvain*: a hero is an animal.

As a dialectical tool, "topic" came to imply the means for finding a missing term in an imperfect argument or enthymeme.[10] As metafiction, topical theory implies either the production or the perception of *conjointure* between two (or more) terms or episodes narrated in a story in such a way that the relationship between them has not been iterated, yet must be grasped (if only intuitively) for the story to be understood. Such is the common feature of narrative *conjointure* (as Chrétien seems to have understood it) and of dialectical topology. *Topics, in short, are those lattent rules of composition which guarantee the possibility of fiction as being formally or logically true without making claims for its being ontologically true*, in the same way as topics allow logicians to construct purely hypothetical syllogisms such as, "if all human beings are wood and all wood is stone, all human beings are stone." Such a statement is a pure fiction—a construction not of the world, but of the mind. It it is surely no accident that poetic fiction should be valorized in the same culture as hypothetical truth that need not be ontologically founded to be true.

Given the dangerous tendency of the *Tristan* story to construct itself as a tissue of lies to which God himself is alleged to be partisan, the idea that poets might find in logic a ground for fiction that is not mendacious was surely a relief. Indeed, is it not possible that poets themselves writing in the twelfth-century propelled such philosophical advances? Is poetic discourse always the passive discourse within a cultural framework? Are poets perhaps not just as provocative for twelfth-century philosophy as they were for Plato and Aristotle?

If we concede the possibility that Chrétien was at least minimally in touch with and partisan to what were by any standards the major intellectual currents of his time, including the ise of dialectics, let us now explore more concretely some possible relations between topical theory and narrative *conjointure* in the story of *Yvain* which summon up in us discriminations of a logical sort: that between substance and accident, and that between true and false contraries. Each of these acts of discrimination involves at least one maximal proposition and a topic, though it was considered above all to be a matter of individual intuition on the part of the dialectician to find the topic most pertinent to the specific propositions which are to be conjoined with proper inference. However, as we see from Boethius's own formation of the topic dealing with contraries, even thought about topical theory tends, for all its abstractness, to evince examples already propitious as material for a good narrative performance:

> The things which Cicero calls contraries are divided into four sorts: adverse contraries, such as white and black; privative contraries, such as justice and injustice; relative contraries, such as master and servant; or negative contraries, such as living and not living. From adverse contraries: if health is good, sickness is bad. From privative contraries: if we flee injustice, we should pursue justice. From relative contraries: whoever wants to be a father should have a child. From negative contraries: you do not accuse me of having done what done what you defend me for not having done [, do you]? The questions have to do with accidents. The maximal proposition: contraries cannot agree with each other when they are adverse, privative, or negative; when they are relative, they cannot occur without each other. The topic: from contraries (which might better be called 'opposites'). (Bk. 3, pp. 66–67)

Obviously in a narrative whose raw material to be conjoined is principally erotic love and chivalric combat, the topic of contraries will implicate both the invention and understanding of most primary human sentiments, as well as of interpersonal relationships (whether martial or erotic) that are manifested there. However, a story, formally speaking, is neither a syllogism nor an enthymeme; therefore, contraries manifested in narrative discourse will tend to be expressed indirectly, reiterated, and sometimes amplified or extended anaphorically over long sequences, even though a single relationship of contrariety continues to pertain. For instance, multiple actions by a single figure or else multiple attributes of a single figure may, by a process of metonymy, come to extend or replace that figure in amplified (yet constant) relationships of contrariety. Moreover, complex stories can combine contraries into larger bundles in which a term of one pair of contraries will become associated with, or even equivalent to, terms of other pairs. Take, for instance, the simple contrary pair animate/inanimate, which is important to the distinction between animal and vegetable. At one point, Yvain lies (almost) inanimate in the forest. He is also unloved. In medieval romance, as in theology, to be lacking in love is to tend toward the lack of life itself, as the tragedy of Tristan and Iseut so clearly showed; here too, an unloved hero has become inanimate. Yvain is suddenly made animate again precisely when the Dame de Noroison's beautiful young damsels enthusiastically rub his naked body with a magic unguent entrusted to them by their mistress. Yvain not only becomes animate (more animate, even, than Roland at Ronceval!) but also becomes loved by a sequence of women leading him back, finally, to his wife Laudine.

Topical theory accounts very well for such substitutions where simple contraries become woven into more complex narrative sequences. Indeed, the following topic, which Boethius calls "incompatibles," may be considered as a useful instrument to account for the amplification of kernel contraries into longer and more complex narrative sequences:

> Incompatibles are consequents of contraries. For example, sleeping and waking are contraries, and snoring is associated with sleepers. So snoring and waking are incompatibles. An argument arises from incompatibles in this way: Do you say that he who snores is awake? The question has to do with accident; it is an argument from incompatibles. The maximal proposition: incompatibles cannot occur together. Again, the Topic from a contrary and [that] from incompatibles seem to be similar, but they are different, because contraries are prima facie opposed to each other, but incompatibles are shown to be opposed to each other by their connection with contraries. For example, sleeping and waking are contrary to each other as they stand; but snoring is incompatible with waking because snoring is connected with sleep. (Bk. 3, pp. 68–71)

Some scholars may very well wish to challenge the suggestion that Chrétien knew about or exploited topical theory (even though it is practically impossible that he did not at least know about it if he had ever heard of dialectics) by the objection that all narrative depends upon some logical premises, just as all people use figures of speech without being rhetoricians. My answer is that he not only exploits the topical foundations of narrative logic, but also tends to *transgress* probable relationships (such as that of contrariety) in such a way as to call attention to them and, finally, to *restore* them. Thus, in Chrétien's fictive universe, the ordinary and probable "relational" contrary of master/servant becomes contextually inverted when Lunette becomes Laudine's "master" (rather, her "mistress") in doctrines of the heart; and the "relational" contrary lord/vassal relationship becomes contextually inverted when Yvain, precisely as he becomes Laudine's lordly husband and defender, also becomes her vassal. The "adverse" contraries of freedom/captivity become contextually inverted as Yvain, shut up in a little chamber from whose window he can gaze upon Laudine, declares his reluctance to leave his "prison" even if the doors were wide open (ll. 1536–40); again, the "adverse" contraries aggressor/defender become reversed when Yvain replaces Esclados in Laudine's household. The "privative" contraries fidelity/infidelity and loved/unloved become temporarily reversed in Yvain's destiny the moment he breaks his promise to return to his wife Laudine after a year of jousting. If critics have long been aware of Chrétien's tendency to make sport of rhetoric even as he exploits it, I suggest that the same spirit of autonomy holds true of his relationship to the discipline of logic.

Perhaps we may generalize and say that in twelfth-century culture, the new virtuosity of vernacular fiction constitutes itself precisely over and against those very laws of necessity and probability that the early scholastics were so carefully asserting in the domain of topical theory, which was the heart of their discipline. Indeed, despite the seeming abstractness and (for us) the remoteness of topical theory, even the artisans of such theory readily provided examples whose concreteness made them eminently useful to the construction of narrative circumstances, both probable and improbable. We have already seen in the case of "contraries" topical examples that can be considered as a kind of "protonarrative," but there is another, even *more* suggestively protonarrative topic, "from associated things," that it is presented by Boethius in such a way that the improbable of the marvelous is already anticipated along with the probable of logic:

> Associated things are those which have a common boundary [*finitimum locum*] so that in time sometimes they go before, as meeting [*congressio*] before love, sometimes they go with the thing with which they are associated, as the noise of footsteps with walking, and sometimes they follow, as mental agitation follows a horrible crime. These things are not . . . necessary even though they happen often. For he who has met [someone] has fallen in love at first sight [with that person]. It is

possible that there be no noise of footsteps when someone is walking; and there can be a noise of footsteps when someone is not walking, if he remains in the same place and moves his feet. Someone can be agitated who has done nothing horrible; and it can be the case that someone who has done something horrible is not agitated.

From these an argument will be drawn when we maintain that someone loves because he had previously met [the person he loved], or that someone walked in a place since the noise of footsteps was heard, or that someone whom we see agitated had committed a horrible crime. In these cases, the questions have to do with accidents. The Topic: from associated things. The maximal proposition: things which are associated with other things are judged on the basis of those things [*ex adjunctis adjuncta perpendi*]. (Bk. 3, p. 67)

The imaginative wealth of Boethius's illustrations of the topic "from associated things" strikes the mind, and a poet such as Chrétien or Marie de France (who both belong to the same intellectual universe) seeking to forge a new narrative poetics could surely have found in such a passage the potential for a half dozen narrative episodes. Both by its examples and by its underlying concept, the topic of "associated things" is reminiscent of Augustine's notion of natural (as opposed to conventional) signs:

Those are natural signs which, without any desire or intention of signifying, make us aware of something beyond themselves, like smoke which signifies fire. It does this without any will to signify, for even when smoke appears alone, observation and memory of experience with things bring a recognition of an underlying fire. The track of a passing animal belongs to this class, and the face of one who is wrathful or sad signifies his emotion even when he does not wish to show that he is wrathful or sad.[11]

However, when Chrétien constructs narrative episodes around premises comparable to those of "associated things," he does so with deftness and humor, and not mechanically. It is by metonymic reasoning similar to that of "associated things" that, when Laudine's servants find the front half of Yvain's horse lying inside the closed gate of Laudine's castle, they quite properly infer that Yvain too must be inside. However, "normal" criteria of associative probability are disrupted when Yvain acquires a magic ring which makes him invisible. Thus, when Esclados's corpse begins spontaneously to bleed, Laudine's servants correctly infer that the slayer is nearby and begin beating with clubs everywhere in the room, except on the bed near the corpse where Yvain, Laudine's future husband, already — and most improbably — lies. Laudine's intense grief over Esclados's death hardly excites the probable response of shared grief or sympathy from his slayer that we would expect in the ordinary world, but rather, her in-

tense grief excites equally intense erotic desire in Yvain. In other words, Chrétien acknowledges ordinary human assumptions of probability in "associated
things," but, like Boethius already was, Chrétien is really more interested in con-
structing scenes where norms of belief are *belied* by circumstances of the exceptional and the marvelous, just as the norms of courtliness are constantly belied
by Keu. As we shall have other occasions to observe, the truth of Chretien's marvelous often begins where logic ends; yet it is precisely this pleasurable transgressive privilege of the poet, this adultery in signs, this irreducible otherness
of fiction — and perhaps of human love as well — with respect to ordinary reality
to which the more steadfast necessities of modal logic apply.

Chapter 5
Si est homo, est animal

It is possible to find many correspondences between dialectical topics and the underlying *conjointures* of Chrétien's narrative syntax—and also, to find conspicuous defiances of topically based truths posed at the narrative surface of Chrétien's fictive universe. For a poet to challenge the established authority of logical discourse is not necessarily to repudiate it, but may be seen as an effective strategy for valorizing the vernacular poetic as an autonomous mode of apprehending reality. Perhaps I may generalize and suggest that no new discourse, poetic or otherwise, can establish itself within a preexisting network of other discourses in a community of speech groups without such provocations or transgressions of established conventions of understanding.

However, the search for topics (like that for rhetorical tropes) can quickly become mechanical and arbitrary; indeed, arbitrariness in the choice of topic to make this or that inference was already acknowledged as a feature of topical theory itself. Therefore, I shall concentrate upon a single topic that is especially important to *Yvain* because it accounts, I believe, for much of the conceptual organization of its story.

The topic is "from kind," and, according to Boethius, its maximal proposition is: "the attributes of genera are observed in their kinds" (Bk. 3, p. 66). Abelard's formulation of this maximal proposition, which we have already encountered in his illustration of his definition of maximal propositions is, as we will recall, "when species is predicated of something, so too is genus" (*De Dialectica*, p. 310), and Abelard gave the following, perfectly classical example of that maximal proposition, "if it is a human, it is an animal." The example is so common in logical treatises all through the Middle Ages that it is a kind of emblem, not only of a train of ideas, but also of philosophical discourse itself. Thus, it is entirely within the realm of possibility, if not of probability, that a poet who is testing the resources of his new vernacular against the prerogatives of logical discourse would start precisely with this commonplace of logical thought.

While a topic such as "from kind" (and its maximal proposition) could aid the dialectician to "find" or to evaluate properly any number of specific but still imperfect arguments, such a topic could also help a narrative poet, first, to invent in his inherited *matière* a kernel story based on the relationship of a human being to his or her generic animality and, second, to amplify that kernel story into a much larger fictive narrative in whose "circumstances" there still pertains, no matter how abundant or various is its content, a coherent structure based on one topical "truth." That is to say, as a narrative poet, Chrétien could find in topical theory a basic grounding for a narrative "truth" that could not only bring new order and form to the traditional *matière* of Celtic and classical legend, but also allow him to integrate into his now-fictive truth contemporary "scientific" thought and ethical values as provided to him by the two other main branches of philosophy (besides that of dialectics): the natural sciences (*physica*) and ethics (*ethica*).

Indeed, I shall claim that such is precisely the case with *Yvain, ou le chevalier au lion*, whose double title already orients us toward the discussion that shall ensue. I shall propose that in this romance Chrétien takes as the basis of his *conjointure* the "special" relationship between a man and his generic animality, and that he expands upon that relationship during a broad sequence of events whose content, for all its diversity, remains conceptually anchored in the topic "from species" as brought to bear upon Yvain as exemplary *homo*. It is precisely this concern for conceptual rigor that marks Chrétien as a late twelfth-century poet whose initiation into *grammatica* would have led him not only into rhetoric, but also into the basics of logic, hence, into topical theory. I shall propose, moreover, that this interpenetration of discourses in Chrétien's time and their condensation into a single poetic text gave rise to what is surely one of the most remarkable statements about humanity and its culture to emerge from twelfth-century humanism.

Let us return, now, to Calogrenant's unfinished quest for an adventure at the beginning of *Yvain*, a quest where success in the contrary (and yet somehow similar) ordeals of love and combat carries the promise of recognition as a courteous and honorable knight in Arthur's court. Seven years ago, we are told, Calogrenant set forth on a quest for an "adventure"("*querant avantures*," l. 177). Not only was Calogrenant young and uninitiated, but he departed "alone like a peasant" ("*seus come paisanz*"), yet fully armed as a knight ("*Armez de totes armeures / Si come chevaliers doit estre*," ll. 178–179). The contrast between Calogrenant's peasant-like solitude and his unproven identity as a knight subsumes not only the opposition between social marginality and social centrality, but also an opposition between states or degrees of being in the human soul. Andreas Cappelanus tells us in his *De amore* (1.11) that peasants are capable only of copulating like mules or horses, and that they merely follow their instinct of desire, instead of loving as full-fledged humans may. Moreover, the peasants should not be prodded to acquire the art of loving because their land would quickly become unproductive. If a noble should desire a peasant, he should not hesitate to possess her by force. Thus, Calogrenant's "peasantry" of soul is that of a man at the bottom threshold of humanity, scarcely above his condition as animal.

Early in his quest in the forest of Broceliande, Calogrenant encounters a horrible peasant ("*vilain*," l. 288), a huge monster of a man carrying a club whose features resemble the parts of many different species of animals (horse, elephant, owl, cat, wolf, boar), the *least* apparent of which is the human species itself, whose principal defining properties are to be rational, capable of speech, and political, that is, inclined to participate in a social order. Moreover, Chrétien generates a sharp conflict, here, between the specific rhetorical conventions of the human portrait[1] and its subhuman animal content. Matter and form enunciate, explictly and implicitly, two different realities—rather, two levels of the same reality, since *si est homo, est animal*. Calogrenant himself is caught in a dilemma of perception and of definition of this creature's exact class or species as animal: can he reason? can he speak?

> Si m'esgarda et mot ne dist
> Ne plus qu'une beste fëist;
> Et je cuidai que il ne eüst
> Reison ne parler ne seüst.
> (ll. 323–26)

Thus he looked at me and did not say a word, any more than might a beast; and I thought that he possessed no reason, and that he did not know how to speak.

Calogrenant nevertheless summons up his courage and addresses the monster, asking him whether he is "a good thing or not," but the monster's answer is perfectly equivocal:

> "Je suis uns hon."
> "Queus hon es tu?" —"Tes con tu voiz.
> Je ne sui autre nule foiz."
> (ll. 330–32)

"I am a man." "What kind of man are you?" "Such as you see: I am never otherwise."

Calogrenant's interlocutor is "man" enough to speak, but he remains ethically undefinable. Were he speaking from his "special" substance as a man, the monster would be either good or bad, or at least sometimes good and sometimes bad; but, given that this monster is always ethically *neither*, the monster is speaking from his subjacent nature as animal, rather than as human, for animals were considered to be subethical beings. Indeed, although the monster has the capacity to speak (and therefore *is* a man), his portrait, in its aggregate, adds up only to *generic* animality and not to *specific* humanness.

There is a topic called "from the whole" which might help us to understand how a portrait like this, as an aggregate of many different species, can be considered as a nonspecific whole, or genus. Boethius says that " 'Whole' generally has two meanings, either genus or complete thing made up of more than one part" (Bk. 2, p. 51). Parts, by contrast, "are those things whose coming together produces the whole. Those things which divide the whole are also called parts, but these are commonly called species or kinds" (Bk. 3, pp. 64–65). This kind of generic whole is opposed to what Abelard calls an "integral" whole (*Dialectica*, p. 547) which, like "Socrates," is unique, and cannot be collective or universal. Nor, says Abelard, is it thinkable that an integral, single substance *in natura* be comprised of the members of different animals (*Dialectica*, p. 548). Although the topic "from the whole" ordinarily leads to the finding of a definition, the monster to whom Calogrenant speaks is a logical *fictio*, who eludes all definition, and for good reason: it is precisely Chrétien's goal in *Yvain* to define human nature as animal , but to do so in narrative, not by logical deduction. Although a man, as animal, may very well embody the attributes of lesser animals (and vice versa, as taught by the bestiaries), and hence, may be intelligent like an elephant, diabolical like a wolf, obedient like a horse, and so forth, what is purposefully lacking in Calogrenant's monstrous interlocutor is precisely that set of *differentiae* that would ordinarily mark him distinctly as a full-fledged member of the human species. It is surprising, perhaps, yet logical, that no hostility is exchanged between Calogrenant and the man-as-animal: the human condition cannot "hold" (*consistere*) without the condition of animality, even though the latter can lack the higher perfection "specific" to the former.

The encounter between Calogrenant and the monster, or man-as-animal, is not, in itself, dialectical in form, since it does not unfold as arguments.[2] Still, this encounter does invite the reader to raise and ponder a hermeneutical question as to the fundamental difference between man-as-human and man-as-animal, and such a question is (whether we are aware of it or not) essentially topical (hence, dialectical). Here, Jean Jolivet, speaking of Abelard, describes the hermeneutical reflex of someone who has been confronted by an argument whose basis of inference is not obvious:

Quand on ne saisit pas immédiatement une inférence, on demande
"d'où est le lieu"—*unde locus?* La forme de cette question montre que
le lieu n'est pas considéré comme substance, mais comme rapport
(*habitudo*); on ne cherche pas à savoir "quelle chose est le lieu" mais
"d'où il est", "c'est-à-dire à quel rapport il doit d'être le nerf de l'inférence" (*ex qua habitudine vim inferentiae teneat*): ainsi, à propos de
l'exemple classique *si est homo est animal*, on ne dit pas que le lieu
est *ab homine*, mais *a specie*; or, "espèce" est bien le nom d'un rapport alors qu' "homme" est le nom d'une substance. (p. 154)

When one does not immediately grasp an inference, one asks, "whence
the place"—*"unde locus?."* The form of that question shows that the
place is not considered as a substance, but as a relationship (*habitudo*):
one does not seek to know "what kind of a thing is the place," but
"from where it comes," that is to say, "in what relationship must it be
the force of inference" (*ex qua habitudine vim inferentiae teneat*).
Thus, regarding the classical example, *si est homo est animal*, one
does not say that the place is *ab homine*, but *a specie*; moreover, "species" is the word for a relationship, while "man" is the word for a substance.

Since Chrétien is a narrative poet and not a dialectician, he does not, of
course, ask *unde locus?*, though Calogrenant's wondering about the monster's
bestial silence and his question to him do reflect a cultural proclivity to perceive
and classify beings in the world by logical criteria that have by now become "natural," even in the vernacular. Chrétien elaborates upon the consequences of the
implied statement underlying this scene, *si est homo, est animal*, not dialectically, but rather in an *ethical* perspective: what exactly is lost, Chrétien invites
us to ponder, when a man as a rational, political animal regresses to his generic
bestiality? For his answers, Chrétien draws upon material from a broad philosophical and literary tradition whose commonplaces, at least, he obviously
knew. For instance, we observe through Calogrenant's astonished eyes that this
"man" is a keeper of fierce and proud bulls which fight with each other in the
forest, and not a keeper of domestic animals grazing peacefully (as they should)
in an enclosed pasture. Chrétien is dramatizing, here, a fundamental antinomy
of wildness and domesticity—and by extension, of nature and culture—that he
has inherited from the classical world (most directly, probably, through Virgil's
Georgics),[3] and Calogrenant himself protests that these bulls have never known
the rule of a man:

> "Que fes tu ci?" "Je m'i estois,
> Si gart cez bestes par cest bois."
> "Gardes? Par saint Pere de Rome!

> Ja ne conoissent eles home
> Ne cuit qu'an plainne an boschage
> Puisse an garder beste sauvage,
> N'an autre leu por nule chose,
> S'ele n'est liiée ou anclose."
>
> (ll. 333–40)

"What are you doing here?" "I stay here and keep these beasts in the forest." "You keep them? By Saint Peter of Rome, they don't know what a man is. I don't think that it is possible to keep a wild beast either in a field or a wilderness, or anywhere else, unless it is tied up or enclosed."

Calogrenant's spontaneous indignation at the man-beast's turning his bulls loose to the wildness of their passions reflects yet deeper ontological assumptions about the nature of man *as* human (as opposed to man as animal). It was common doctrine among virtually all of the major classical and Christian currents to which Chrétien could possibly have been heir to distinguish between three levels of soul in living creatures: the vegetative, the animal, and the human. The vegetative soul is capable of generation and growth, but is without sense or intelligence. The animal soul, which cannot hold or "consist" without the vegetative, is capable of generation, growth, and motion, and is sensible, but is limited to appetition, which is to say that it responds directly to what it perceives passively through the senses. These responses are passions, and they fall into two basic categories: wrath or fear (*ira*, or *metu*), and desire (*libido, concupiscentia, cupiditas*), though in reality, wrath and fear are really subclasses of desire: that is, we react in anger or fear because we desire to be happy.[4] The human soul subsumes the lower powers of both the vegetative and the animal, yet possesses the differential faculty of reason, whose purpose is to govern these basic passions and to lead humankind to higher wisdom.[5] Hugh of St. Victor summarizes this hierarchy of faculties:

> But the third power of the soul appropriates the prior nutritional and sense-perceiving powers, using them, so to speak, as domestics and servants. It is rooted entirely in the reason, and it exercises itself either in the most unfaltering grasp of things present, or in the understanding of things absent, or in the investigation of things unknown. This power belongs to humankind alone. It not only takes in sense impressions and images which are perfect and well founded, but, by a complete act of the understanding, it explains and confirms what imagination has only partially suggested. (*Didascalicon* 1.3)

Hugh also makes it clear that the faculty of reason, which is proper to humankind alone, is meant to prevail over the animal soul of humans: "For while the nature of brute animals, governed by no rational judgment, produces movements guided only by a certain blind inclination of the flesh, it remains true that the actions of the rational soul are not swept away by blind impulses, but are always preceded by Wisdom as their guide" (1.4). Hugh's model of mind is as political as it is psychological, reflecting a strong tendency of classical and medieval (and perhaps modern) cultures to find models of mind and of government that are homologous, if not identical.[6] Tyrants are rulers who, by definition, dispense with law and justice in order to rule by policy and by fear, becoming at the same time slaves of their own bestial passions. Such Platonic and Aristotelian doctrines were commonplaces of medieval culture as well, thanks not only to Cicero, but also to Aristotle himself whose political theories were once again becoming current in Chrétien's time.[7] Though he wrote after Chrétien, here is how Thomas Aquinas, following both Aristotle and Cicero, describes tyranny:

> Tyrannical government is based exclusively upon fear; and tyrants seek by every means to make themselves feared by their subjects. But fear makes a weak foundation. For those who remain subjects through fear will, when opportunity and the hope of success presents itself, rise up against those who command them: and the rising up will be the more violent the more they have been constrained against their will, and through fear alone.[8]

If we may see the wild bulls fighting in the forest as unambiguous emblems of unbridled passion, the man-beast himself is hardly a notch higher in the order of being, for he "governs" not by reason, but by the "justice" of his own brute passion. Just as the tyrant makes a law of his or her own personality, so too the man-beast boasts that

> "N'i a celi, qui s'ost movoir,
> Des qu'eles me voient venir."
> (ll. 344–45)

"There's not a one that dares moves as soon as they see me come."

Moreover, fear is the sole basis of the man-beast's "lordship" over his beasts. At a time when medieval culture was debating actively about the nature and limits of legitimate political power in a feudal framework, surely the ideological resonances of Chrétien's portrait of the man-beast's tyrannical dominion over his bulls could not have passed unnoticed:

> "Car quand j'en puis une tenir,
> Si la destraing par les deus corz
> As poinz, que j'ai et durs et forz,

Que les autres de peor tranblent
. . . .
Einsi sui de mes bestes sire."
(ll. 346–55)

"For, when I catch one of them, I grab him by both horns with my rough, tough hands, and the others tremble with fear. . . .   Thus am I lord of my beasts."

It is, I hope, clear by now that Chrétien is "inventing" a story whose narrative surface is subtended by a deep relational truth bearing upon the generic animal basis of the human species, and we will hopefully recognize the "topical" basis of that truth. Moreover, a topical apprehension of the relationship between genus and species can give rise to multiple descriptions and narrative episodes whose material is highly eclectic and diverse, yet whose logic of *narrative* antecedent and consequence remains perfectly coherent and stable. Thus, if a man as species is reasonable, a man as mere animal is lacking in reason; if a man as species is naturally social and law abiding, a man as mere animal lives by tyranny without law, and so forth. Moreover, any of these subjects, in turn, is susceptible to amplification in accordance with social doctrines and customs familiar to Chrétien and his twelfth-century intellectual milieu. Since philosophy was hardly a homogeneous corpus or discipline in Chrétien's time, it must have been an intellectual challenge for him as artist to amplify a topically conceived narrative "argument" with nondialectical substance drawn from the multiple sources at his disposal. Thus, if a man is by definition a reasonable animal, it follows that Chrétien will tend to express, in his man-beast, a creature deprived of all those qualities which are associated (by "associated things"?) with humankind's "special" faculty of reason.

Indeed, by Chrétien's time, the province of human reason had come to include many different modes of action. Thus, if philosophy had always been considered, since Plato, as the highest manifestation of the human capacity to reason, philosophy in twelfth-century Aristotelianism had been expanded by Hugh of St. Victor to include all human actions falling into three basic categories, the "theoretical," the "practical," and the "mechanical." The theoretical includes logic, mathematics, and physics; the practical is divided into ethics, economics, and politics; mechanical philosophy includes seven skills: weaving, armament, commerce, agriculture, hunting, medicine, and "theatrics," or *scientia ludorum* (*Didascalicon*, Bok. 2).

We should not be surprised to observe that, given his status of a man as mere animal, Calogrenant's savage interlocutor should lack in most of these accoutrements of human reason. Although he can speak, the man-beast is quite obviously remote from the abstract theoretical arts. (However, since Chrétien's noble patrons were probably, themselves, quite unversed in these arts as well, Chrétien surely knew that it was not in his interest to play that register too loudly.) In things practical, we have already seen that the man-beast is cruel, undomesticated, and tyrannical, hence, totally at odds with what is properly ethical, economic, and political.

The man-beast's grades in the mechanical arts are also very low. Instead of wearing artifacts of woven textile, he wears skins that have been torn from freshly killed animals and then not even cured or tanned. Instead of bearing a sword, he either fights with his fist like a primitive human, or he wields a club that, in a chivalric perspective, is the "minimal" weapon and is linked to the iconographical convention of the wild man.[9] Instead of laboring in the agricultural world of field and pasture, the man-beast inhabits the forest. If we may think of the telling of *avantures* in the courtly feast as the closest thing in twelfth-century secular aristocratic culture to the now defunct tradition of classical "theatrics," then we should not expect much of the man-beast on that score either, since he does not even understand the meaning of the word *avanture*, from which heroic stories spring. As for the three remaining skills of commerce, hunting, and medicine, Chrétien will deal with these later in his story when Yvain himself will regress from his human perfection as a knight and as a lover to the generic state of wild animal in the forest.

In his dialogue with the man-as-animal in the forest (which is also a dialogue with himself), Calogrenant opens with a question that remains unresolved during their encounter: whether the man-as-animal is a " 'good thing or not' " (" '*Va, car me di, / Se tu es buene chose ou non!*' ", ll. 328–29). Even though we are shown here many potentially negative aspects of a man's behavior when he reverts to his generic status as animal (and such negative aspects are borne out later by Yvain), Calogrenant and the man-beast, as I have noted, are scarcely hostile to each other: to the contrary, one is curious and the other obliging. I would suggest that Chrétien deliberately leaves Calogranant's question open, not only because it is to remain an active one throughout the rest of the story, but also because it reflects an unresolved ethical question that lies at the very heart of a new vernacular culture trying to square off with the conflicting messages of antiquity: is passion a legitimate motive for truly heroic action? Can or should men and women whose honor is rooted in an ideal of action (whether in chivalric combat or in love) strive to eliminate from their souls those generic appetites of desire and wrath or fear that humans have in common with other animals?

Chrétien's culture had inherited contradictory classical and Christian attitudes toward human passion. On the negative side were the teachings of the Stoics, transmitted to the Middle Ages largely by Cicero, who felt that passion could *never* be the motive of proper ethical action.[10] Alongside these were the Neoplatonic doctrines of Plotinus, who taught that evil in the human soul stems from passions that assault it through its corporeality (*Enneades* 1.8). Both of these negative traditions converged in the "philosophical" Augustine of the *De libero arbitrio*, which was written shortly after his discovery of Neoplatonism and his conversion and which taught that the fall of the human soul occurs through *libido* (which includes all other passions, including anger and fear) caused by the soul's chosen attachment to matter (1.3.8; 1.5.11; 1.11.21). In the *De trinitate* 12.11, Augustine sees bestiality in humans as a punishment for pride:

> For the true honour of man is the image and likeness of God, which is not preserved except be it in relation to Him by whom it is impressed. The less therefore that one loves what is one's own, the more one cleaves to God. But through the desire of making trial of his own power, man by his own bidding falls down to himself as to a sort of intermediate grade. And so, while he wishes to be as God is, that is, under no one, he is thrust on, even from his own middle grade, by way of punishment, to that which is lowest, that is, to those things in which beasts delight: and thus, while his honour is the likeness of God, but his dishonour is the likeness of the beast, "Man being in honour abideth not; he is compared to the beasts 18 that are foolish, and is made like to them" (Psalm 49).[11]

On the positive side, there was a tradition affirming human passion that stemmed from Plato's *Phaedrus*, in which Socrates describes his love of spiritual things as a veritable frenzy. The soul, he says, is like a charioteer (reason) borne aloft by winged horses (the appetites), and though these must be disciplined by the reins of reason, they must not be annihilated so that we become nonlovers of divine Truth. This Platonic tradition *also* reached Augustine, that is, the Augustine marked by Ambrose and the more dynamic and mystical Augustine of the *Confessions* who is propelled toward spiritual ascendance by passions of the most intense and personal sort. As Erich Auerbach has said, it was this passionate side of the Christian faith, modelled on the passion of Christ himself, that prevailed during the early Middle Ages and flowered with renewed intensity in the spiritual life of the twelfth century.[12] But there was another positive tradition, a more rational one stemming mainly from Aristotle, which was now also making deep inroads into Chrétien's culture, even though we cannot specify exactly which Aristotelian doctrines Chrétien himself knew, or how *directly* he knew them. Aristotle insisted positively upon the link between appetition (that is, the soul's susceptiblity to passion) and movement, hence, between emotion and motion (*motus*) (*De anima* 3.10). Humans are animals, and their very capacity to move is coextensive with the appetitive self; it follows, therefore, that a deficiency of anger is just as dangerous to the well-being of the soul as an excess:

With regard to anger, also, there is an excess, a deficiency, and a mean. Although they can scarcely be said to have names, yet since we call the intermediate person good-tempered, let us call the mean good temper; of the persons at the extremes let the one who exceeds be called irascible, and his vice irascibility, and the man who falls short an irascible sort of person, and the deficiency inirascibility.[13]

Although Chrétien shows himself receptive to each of these currents at different moments of his poetic career, in Yvain he valorizes passion beginning at its most elementary level. As Jean Frappier has noted, Calogrenant first finds the path to chivalric adventure through the good offices of the man-beast who points out the way to the magic fountain.[14] Chrétien thereby confirms the existential primacy of a man's animal and passional nature as a generic substratum for his more perfectable, "special" humanity. The manbeast is more a neutral emanation of Calogrenant's (and every person's) generic animal nature than his enemy; hence, they do not fight. Since beasts are not properly ethical beings,[15] the man-beast cannot possibly know what is the proper ethical or political end of human passion, much less the meaning of the word *avanture*, which implies the carrying of human passion to its highest perfection; however, the man-beast does at least know something about the *inception* of passion, for instance, what marvelous things happen to young *bacheliers* in the forest when liquid from the basin is spilled on the rock beside the fountain. In *Yvain*, more than in any other of his romances, Chrétien remains very close to human passion as an elementary force in the material world and seems preoccupied above all with the question, more ethical than religious, of how primitive human desire may be transmuted into a broader economy of desire. We may perhaps see two contrasting symbols in the basin whose liquid a hero spills upon a rock and in the magic fountain beside it: the first, the basin, stresses the primary, accidental eroticism of youth that leads through violent disruption back to primeval chaos; the second, or the fountain, stresses upward movement in stasis, which is the noble man's goal as a married lover of a woman who, like Enide, is both mistress and spouse. It is this second idea that best corresponds to twelfth-century doctrines of perfection of matter in form, of passion in reason, and this is the natural *telos* of Yvain's human desires as well.

Chrétien's positive recognition of the primacy of human passion as the raw material of responsible human action is expressed not only in the relationship between a man and his generic animal substratum, but also in that spatial opposition between the aristocratic court (understood as the *locus* of human perfection) and the forest. The legacy of *Romanitas* had offered to Chrétien a clearcut opposition between the city and the forest as *loci*, respectively, of law or reason and of bestial passion: for instance, Dido and Aeneas fornicated in a cave in the forest, and their passion subverted the same Carthage that Dido as queen and lawgiver had been conscientiously building when the Trojans first arrived on her shore. Moreover Servius, Virgil's second-century commentor, glosses the forest in *Aeneid* 6 as "dens of darkness, in which rage and lust hold sway."[16] In Chrétien, by contrast, the wood is a place where a man's elementary, passional self is first summoned forth in its fullest range of expression, and this aspect of a man's nature as *potency* is indispensable to that ultimate perfection of his being in the arts of chivalric warfare and courteous love.

Indeed, Chrétien's tendency to see the forest as a locus of primeval human passion which seeks its own perfection in order and form is a fictive restatement of broader contemporary platonic attitudes toward the forest (*silva*) as a metaphor for matter. In Bernard Sylvester's *Cosmographia, Silva* as "wood" personifies the ancient Greek concept of matter as "wood found in the forests" which lends itself to the constructions of things such as houses. Already in Greek thought, the concept had become generalized:

> The original definite "content" *wood*, disappears; only the idea of the function the wood plays in building is maintained and extended to every similar or analogous item. Now, if we ask what kind of function is meant here, the general answer seems to be: the function of being that (indeterminate) out of which something can be made. In a more abstract way, we could say: the availability, the plasticity, the determinability which is presupposed to every action of making something. Productive action is conceived as working on a given "material", which presents a "possibility" of being shaped in a definite way. Here we seem to have the origin of the conception which sees matter as potency. Matter appears here primarily as correlative to productive action: that out of which something is made. In this context, the relation between matter and the active principle has a certain priority to the relation between matter and "form".[17]

In Bernard, *Silva* or *Hyle* is matter endowed with a will to perfection achievable through form: "*Silva*, intractable, a formless chaos, hostile coalescence, the motley appearance of being, a mass discordant with itself, longs in her turbulence for a tempering power; in her crudity, for form; in her rankness, for cultivation. Yearning to emerge from her ancient confusion, she demands the shaping influence of number and the bonds of harmony."[18] However, *Silva* is also inclined, through a certain *malignitas*, to resist the imposition of form and must be refined by Noys, or the eternal reason of God: "Now Hyle exists in an ambiguous state, suspended between good and evil, but because her evil tendency preponderates, she is more readily inclined to acquiesce in its impulses" (p. 69). Bernard is emphatic about the primacy of *Silva* or *Hyle* to created beings:

> Hyle was Nature's most ancient manifestation, the inexhaustible womb of generation, the primary basis of formal existence, the matter of all

bodies, the foundation of substance. Her capaciousness, confined by no boundaries or limitations, extended itself from the beginning to such vast recesses and such scope for growth as the totality of creatures would demand. And since diverse and intricate qualities pervaded her, the matter and foundation of their perpetuity, she could not but be thrown into confusion, for she was assailed in such manifold ways by all natural existence. (p. 70)

Given the morally ambigous nature of the man-beast, given his composite identity made up of multiple species of animal, given his disdain to confine and pacify his passionate, warring bulls, and given, finally, his own servitude to passion, we may understand, now, why this generic animal (whose being subtends our own) should inhabit the *silva* of Broceliande. Moreover, Bernard Sylvester himself mentions the very same forest of Broceliande as one of the most prominent and memorable forests of the creation, along with those of Greece and Asia (*Cosmographia* 1.3). I shall speak more about historical forests and romance later. Suffice it for the moment to suggest that Chrétien probably saw a connection between *Silva* as cosmic matter to be perfected by divine authority through form and his own historical relationship as author to the pre-existing, but disparate, tangle of ancient *matière* to which he, as a *litteratus* also embued with the power of reason, will bring *sens* as the *domus* of perfected poetic form.[19]

Although Yvain enlists himself to perfect Calogrenant's confused story, his initial success only leads to yet graver human failures than those of Calogrenant, and I would suggest that a specifically topical concern with a representative man's relationship to his generic animal nature *continues* to govern both the content of the episodes in the romance and their *conjointure*. Yvain's problem (unlike Calogrenant's) is not one of summoning up sufficient force of body and mind to bring to conclusion an adventure of love and war, but rather one of maintaining the proper measure or economy of passions in his soul. During the wedding festivities for Yvain and Laudine, Gauvin admonishes Yvain not to become one of those knights " 'who are diminished by their wives' " (" *'qui por lor fames valent mains,'* " l. 2486), and he prevails upon Yvain to augment his knightly honor by questing after new adventures. Yvain must avoid, in other words, the shame that beset Erec when he neglected his chivalry through overindulgence in love following his marriage with Enide. Yvain's passion for chivalric honor is in itself laudable, but only so long as it is kept within measure. Although Chrétien recognizes, and even applauds, the transgressive and anarchic nature of human passion in its initial phases, *moderatio* is ultimately the key to virtue in the human disciplines of love and war. Even Laudine herself readily consents to Yvain's departure on a quest, but only for a specific period, limited to one year's time.

When Yvain's thirst for chivalric honor becomes so unreasonable that he forgets his promise to Laudine, this once proud hero begins to regress to the lowest limits of his animal soul. While Calogrenant's encounter with his generic animal nature had been a necessary point of departure on a path toward *avanture* leading (at least potentially) to human perfection, Yvain's regression from human perfection back to generic animality, which begins the instant when Lunette reminds him of his truancy, is totally degrading. Moreover, his regression is systematic, by which I mean that Chrétien carefully programs Yvain's divestment of all his principal traits as "man" as he regresses to his primitive animal state. In other words, Chrétien is now giving new *ethical* substance to the topic "from species" stating that "if it is a human, it is an animal."

Since speech is one of the most obvious *differentiae* of human beings as species, it should come as no surprise that the first property that Yvain loses when Lunette demands the return of the ring that Laudine had given him at their wedding is, precisely, his faculty of speech:

> "Yvains, n'a mes cure de toi
> Ma dame, ainz te mande par moi
> Que ja mes vers li ne revaingnes
> Ne son anel plus ne detaingnes.
> Par moi, que ci an presant vois,
> Te mande que tu li anvois.
>
> . . . .
>
> Yvains respondre ne li puet,
> Que sans et parole li faut."
>
> (ll. 2767–76)

"Yvain, my mistress no longer loves you; thus, she orders you through me that you never return to her and that you keep her ring no longer. She orders that through me, whom you see here before you, you send it back to her." . . . Yvain could not answer her, for both thought and speech failed him.

The second property of his species that Yvain loses is sociability, for humans are also by definition social or political animals: Yvain is now so ashamed of himself that he decides to flee all human company into the wilderness:

> Mis se voldrait estre a la fuie
> Toz seus an si sauvage terre,
> Qe l'an ne le seust ou querre,
> N'ome ne fame n'i eüst
> Ne nus de lui rien ne seüst
> Ne plus que s'il fust an abisme.
>
> (ll. 2784–89)

He wished to flee all alone into such a wilderness that they would not even know where to look for him, so that not a man, woman, nor anyone at all, would know any more about him even if he fell into an abyss.

The third property of the human species that Yvain loses is the power of reason, and as reason departs, Yvain tears up his clothes. Cloth-making, one will recall, was the first of the mechanical arts in Hugh of St. Victor's *Didascalicon*.

> Et il va tant que il fu loing
> Des tantes et des paveillons.
> Lors li monta uns torbeillons
> El chief si granz que il forsane,
> Lors se descire et se depane
> Et fuit par chans et par arees.
>
> (ll. 2802–7)

And he goes until he was far from the tents and pavillions. Then so great a whirlpool went to his head that he went insane, and he ripped and tore off his clothes and fled through the fields and ploughlands.

The next two mechanical arts to fall into decline are those of armament and commerce (which are second and third in Hugh's order of presentation), for Yvain substitutes the lowly peasant's bow for the nobler arms of knighthood when he steals (rather than purchases) a bow and some arrows from a young peasant boy. At last, Yvain wanders naked through the forest and stalks wild animals, whose flesh he eats "completely raw," exactly as other predatory animals do:

> au garçon
> Est alez tolir son arçon
> Et les saietes qu'il tenoit.
> Por ce mes ne li sovenoit
> De nule rien, qu' il eüst feite
> Les bestes par le bois agueite,
> Si les ocit et si manjue
> La veneison trestote crue.
>
> (ll. 2819–26)

He went to the boy and snatched his bow and the arrows that he was holding. He no longer remembered anything more that he had done. He stalks the beasts in the forest, and kills them and eats their flesh completely raw.

Yvain's conduct as primitive hunter eating his food "completely raw," as other predatory animals do, represents a decline of the fifth mechanical art, *venatio*, which includes both the art of hunting and the culinary arts. The culinary arts contain two principal subdivisions, the baking of bread, which is the most fundamental of all nourishment, and the cooking of *obsonium*, or that which is eaten with bread, a term that Jerome Taylor translates as "side dishes." Here is how Hugh defines *venatio*:

> Hunting is divided into gaming, fowling, and fishing . . . Its name, however, is taken from only one part of it because in antiquity men used to eat merely by hunting, as they still do in certain regions where the use of bread is extremely rare, where flesh is the only food and water or mead the drink.
> Food (*cibus*) is of two kinds—bread and side dishes. Bread (*panis*) takes its name either from the Latin word for one's laying a thing out (*ponis*), or from the Greek word for all (*pan*), because all meals need bread in order to be well provided . . . Hunting, therefore, includes all the duties of bakers, butchers, cooks, and tavern keepers. (p. 77)

Divested, now, of reason and of all its attributes, especially mastery of the mechanical arts, Yvain has regressed so far to his generic animal state that he is at the zero point of his humanity.

If Chrétien has systematically rehearsed all of the main properties of the human species that have been lost in this portrait of regression, he no less systematically depicts Yvain's *return* to humanity, to chivalry, to love, and finally to the court. Yvain's first renewal of contact with his species occurs when he happens upon the hut of a hermit who is clearing land in the forest. It is interesting that Yvain, a "crazed and wild man" (*"hon forsenez et sauvage,"* l. 2828), should meet, of all people, a man of God in the forest who is also scarcely "human," but in a different way: one is bestial and subrational; the other is spiritual and suprarational; yet both are penitent. Why should these two apolitical, nonspeaking men meet in the forest? An answer, may perhaps be found, once again, in Aristotelian political philosophy, which was making its way back into the West and which held that an apolitical man is either morally inferior or else morally superior to the normal man.[20] Although it is anachronistic with regard to Chrétien, the following passage from Aquinas's commentary on Aristotle's *Politics* is perhaps pertinent, even as hindsight, to this meeting of Yvain and the hermit:

> But if a man is such that he is not political on account of nature, either he is bad, as when this happens as a result of the corruption of human nature, or he is better than man, namely in so far as he has a nature more perfect than that generally found in other men, in such a way that by himself he can be self-sufficent without the company of

men, as was the case with John the Baptist and Blessed Anthony the hermit.[21]

This encounter delineates not only the upper and lower thresholds of humanity, but also a threshold of the economic world as well, for the hermit is clearing land, that is, reestablishing those very same, fundamental limits between nature and culture that previously had been effaced by the man-beast keeping his bulls unenclosed in the primitive forest.

Although it is possible to find learned explanations for what first appears to be a curious accident in the historical forest of Broceliande, I would suggest that Chrétien's story was also touching, in the encounter between Yvain and the hermit, on ideological points whose direct historical pertinence was what could have motivated such an exploitation of classical source material in the first place. The twelfth century was a period of considerable demographic expansion which entailed an ecological rebalancing of the realms of agriculture and the uncultivated "desert," and, in more general terms, a new and unRoman perception of the relationship between nature and culture based on complementarity, rather than antithesis. According to Georges Duby, the expansion of fields for the cultivation of grain and for pastures became intense of the beginning of the twelfth century, with the initiative of both the peasants and the lords.[22] However, the infringement of agriculture on seigneurial forests demanded a compromise: now the need for forest reserves necessary to abundance in the art of hunting, so important to the aristocratic sense of its identity as a class, competed with increased motive of agricultural profit in a world of expanding markets (p. 148). It is interesting that Chrétien has chosen a hermit, and not a profitmotivated peasant, as an exemplary land-clearer. Duby says that hermits in the twelfth century were indeed engaged in the process of clearing land, though monks were not (pp. 146–47).

Yvain's first encounter with this other perfectly marginal member of his species is at first absolutely minimal, and involves neither speech nor any other signmaking activity proper to humans as social animals, but merely the taking of a piece of bread left out for him by the hermit. However, since bread is a nutrient derived from grain that has been harvested, ground, and cooked by the industrious hand of a human, and is not something merely gathered by foraging in the wild, we may say that a threshold back into humanity has been crossed, though *barely*: not only is the bread moldy, dry, and sour, but it is made of barley mixed with chaff.[23] Like Chaucer, whose Wife of Bath equates her low social status with barley bread, and whose Prioresse feeds white bread to her classy dogs, Chrétien probably sees different kinds of bread as emblems of social and moral states. (Hugh of St. Victor mentions, for his part, eleven different types of bread in his description of the mechanical art *venatio*.) That Yvain relishes this strictly minimal fare of bread and water as if it were a banquet of meats and fine sauces is a poignant indication not only of how hungry he is, but also of how alienated he is from his proper habitat among the knights and noble ladies of his species:

> N'avoit mie cinc souz costé
> Li sestiers, don fu fez li pains,
> Qui plus iert egres que levains,
> D'orge pestriz atot la paille,
> Et avuec ce iert il sanz faille
> Moisiz et ses come une une escorce.
> Mes li fains l'angoisse et esforce
> Tant que le pout li sot li pains;
> Qu'a toz mangiers est sausse fains
> Bien destanpree et bien confite.
> Tot manja le pain a l'ermite
> Mes sire Yvains, que buen li sot,
> Et but de l'eve froide au pot.
>
> (ll. 2846–58)

The batch of bread did not cost five sous, and was more sour than yeast. It was made with barley mixed with straw, and was moldy all over and dry as bark. But hunger distresses him and the bread pleased him as if it were stew, for hunger is like a sauce to any food and makes it seem well blended and prepared. My lord Yvain ate all the bread, which seemed good to him, and drank the cold water from the bowl.

Because of the contradiction between his antisocial asceticism and his surprisingly deft economic initiative, Chrétien's hermit raises fascinating problems, both historical and methodological, for the modern critic. The hermit stands in obvious counterpoint with the man-beast at the beginning of the romance. The latter is a portrait of the generic animality of humans; he dominates his beasts by tyrannical passion in a thick forest full of brambles and thorns (ll. 181–83). The man-beast is more *sub*ethical than he is evil, to the extent that his generic being is ontologically prior to the human species (understood as the perfection of animate creatures) exactly as the forest is prior to the ethical perfection of the court, or even as the *matière* is to the *sens* of the tale. I am using the term "perfection" here in an etymological, and more medieval, sense: *perficio* means, among other things, to "achieve," "dispatch," "finish," or "complete." For instance, Augustine, in his *De Genesi ad litteram*, describes the creation of the cosmos through the Trinity as a process of "perfection" which occurred with the turning or the "conversion" of matter to God, at which time the different species became distinct (*ita et in conuersione at perfectione creaturae, utrerum species* *digerantur*, 1.6.12). Because humans are both corporeal and spiritual, and because they are also endowed with free will, humans have the potential to sink lower than any other being, or, as Aristotle says, to become the worst of all animals[24] – as does Yvain when he sins against his love for Laudine. Yvain becomes ethically worse than the man-beast because he has denied (as the man-beast has not) the good that is in him.

The hermit, by contrast, represents the "special" perfection of humans as spiritual creatures. He has rejected ordinary human society as his standard of perfection in order to assume, in a gesture of supreme penitence, the guilt of the cosmos from its most rudimentary forms. He tests his own individual goodness by centering his charity wholly upon the love of God, rather than by squandering it on humans. The man-beast is asocial and subrational; the hermit is asocial and suprarational, to the extent that he has rejected even the religious community of the monastery and a life of learning for solitary meditation of the most immediate and passionate sort. Together, then, the man-beast and the hermit represent the lower and upper limits of a human hierarchy.

Chrétien's hermit is more, however, than a pure man of God in the forest: to our surprise, he also turns out to be quite a man of the world. When Yvain begins to lay game at the hermit's door, thereby reciprocating *quid pro quo*, as even animals can, the material charity of the hermit, an interesting recovery from bottom-line depression (both spiritual and economic), begins. From this primitive barter system a more complex system of exchange now spontaneously arises, one that supposes a division of labor, the accumulation of surplus, the mobility of commodities, the intervention of middlemen, and the monetarization of the exchange value of things to be exchanged.[25] Thus, the hermit skins the game that Yvain brings him (suggesting, perhaps that the hermit has known the noble art of *venatio* first hand), he cooks the meat, he takes the hides to market in town where he sells them, he buys barley and oats, he bakes bread in more abundance (unleavened though it still is), and he shares this bread with a hungry, yet productive Yvain.

This fascinating little vignette about the "origins" of commerce in the elementary charity of a forest hermitage calls for closer attention. What conceivable set of assumptions, we may ask, could have led Chrétien to link nascent commercial initiative with a hermit? There is an obvious answer to this question, which is that the hermit's motive of *charity* in the process of exchange set him up as an ideal model for commercial exchange that is not built on *cupidity*. In this sense, the hermit's motives stand diametrically opposed to the profit motive of the merchant, at least as that figure is caricatured by Chrétien himself in *Guillaume d'Angleterre*. In this romance, according to Emanuel J. Mickel,

Throughout the text the merchant class is made to represent the material life, a bestial existence focused only on material gain . . . The merchant sets as his goal the acquisition of wealth, and everything he does is calculated to further him along the path to riches and independence. He is the epitome of the man who wishes to be the master of his own condition, and has no other values than profit, and never even considers values which take no account of gain. Thus, the father of Lovel gives the son the best advice he knows in sending him into the world: "*Ja n'arestés / En liu, ce vos los et enseng,/ Se vos n'i veés vo gaeng.*" ["Don't stop anywhere, I advise and instruct you, if you see no gain there."][26]

Although much has been made by modern historians of the caricatural antimercantilism of the church throughout the Middle Ages, this official policy, which Chrétien himself sometimes echoes (as Mickel has shown), must not be allowed to blind us to important countercurrents, both pragmatic and ideological, in the very same culture, especially in Chrétien's Champagne, and even in Chrétien's own writing as well. As I mentioned earlier, Hugh of St. Victor positively valorizes commerce as one of the seven mechanical arts. Hugh's description of the art of commerce gives us some interesting clues, moreover, about the logic behind the meeting in *Yvain* between a ruined and depraved aristocratic knight and a hermit in the forest from which new prosperity, spiritual as well as material, arises.

First of all, Hugh's description of commerce confers a quasi-heroic and almost noble status on the figure of the merchant. Furthermore, the merchant's wanderings in the mysterious hinterlands are strikingly similar to the chivalric *aventure* into the marvels of the wilderness:

> Commerce contains every sort of dealing in the purchase, sale and exchange of foreign goods. This art is beyond all doubt a peculiar sort of rhetoric — strictly of its own kind — for eloquence is in the highest degree necessary to it. Thus the man who excels others in fluency of speech is called a *Mercurius*, or Mercury, as being a *mercatorum kirrius* (= *kyrios*) — a very lord among merchants. Commerce penetrates the secret places of the world, approaches shores unseen, explores fearful wildnernesses, and in tongues unknown and with barbaric peoples carries on the trade of mankind. The pursuit of commerce reconciles nations, calms wars, strengthens peace, and commutes the private good of individuals into common benefit of all. (*Didascalicon* 2.23)

Hugh is an early spokesman for a movement that grew to considerable proportions during the twelfth century, especially as Chrétien's pations Henri-le-libéral and Marie de Champagne became energetic patrons of a burgeoning international commerce. It is well known that by their carefully policed and regulated commercial fairs they managed to make of Champagne the trade center of Western Europe during the second half of the twelfth century.[27] Therefore, one can imagine that Chrétien's patrons must have enjoyed this cheery little story about the origins, in Broceliande, of their own marvelous economy. All that Yvain's meat lacks is spices from the Orient, and they are on the way.

Despite the apparent simplicity of this allegorical "origin" of commerce in the encounter between an insane knight and a hermit in the woods, more needs to be said both about the historical implications of Chrétien's gesture and about our own way of *describing* it. In a recent article, whose concerns with the economic substratum of courtly discourse overlap with previous studies of my own, Peter Haidu has made the following remarks about the hermit episode—remarks with which, for the most part, I agree:

> The text makes a number of assumptions here. It assumes the hermit's differentiation of Yvains's kills into the edible and the inedible, the meat and the leather. It assumes that the hermit skins the animals and puts aside the skins as a primitive accumulation of capital. It assumes a trip to another place, then, in which the leather is exchanged—in another exchange pattern, a commercial one now—for another object that is desired, namely, a better grade of bread than is appropriate to a religious solitary. It assumes, then, a social differentiation by the hermit between his own status and that of the knight, recognized, inspite of his madness and nakedness, as belonging to another social class. It assumes, finally, the existence of a nearby place of commercial exchange—a town or village—settled by a group of men living in society, as opposed to the solitary's eremitical life, and the possibility, apparently ever-present, of plugging into its economic system.[28]

Haidu continues his argument by proposing that the hermit episode depicts a "closed" economy" whose "functioning" is "metaphorical," and that the juxtaposition, by metonymy, of this closed economy with the "open economy" of the town amounts to the "deconstruction" of the former by the latter:

> The social system of Yvain and the hermit represents a small, local, independent unit of production continguous to the social system functioning at its edges. The principle of contiguity is the necessary presupposition of the text's juxtaposition of two fictional worlds. It is only thanks to this metonymic contiguity that both the metaphoric, closed system of the hermit's world and the open commercial world of generalized exchange can be presented diegetically. As contiguity, its functioning is metonymical, in opposition to the metaphorical functioning of the hermit diegesis proper. This lateral, associative textual move is the opposite pole of textual functioning from the substitutive metaphorical structure preceding. As such, it represents the deconstruction of the former. (p. 135)

Although I find a curious disjunction of level in Haidu's argument, it does draw critical attention to questions concerning both the purely internal dynamics of Chrétien's textual performance and the interplay of social codes that are implicated in the diegetic world Chrétien's narrative. I would suggest, though, that Haidu's argument, for all its subtlety and its claim for historical validity, calls for certain modifications based precisely upon a yet more historical understanding of the hermit's peculiar pattern of conduct. As a historical type, the twelfth-century hermit was an extremely ambiguous figure. On the one hand, traditional Benedictine monasticism allowed for hermitism as a legitimate spiritual state,[29] amd monastic orders still actively remembered their origins in Christ's sojourn in the desert and in the exemplary hermitism of later figures such as Saints Anthony and Jerome.[30] Thus, hermitages were commonly authorized to form in the lands surrounding established monasteries, and their figures were accepted as the pure among the pure.

In one sense, then, the figure of the hermit might seem like a good emblem for extreme "closedness" of all sorts, including those of the economy (as Haidu argues) and of the cloister itself. Indeed, hermitism could lead right back into monastic reform. To give two important examples, Bruno of Cologne founded the Carthusian order in 1084,[31] and Robert D'Arbrissel founded the famous Abbey of Fontrevaux in 1099.[32] Moreover, hermits were hardly social rejects, since the majority of them were noble (despite Haidu's contrary claims for the hermit in Yvain) and *litterati*,[33] as is, for example, the hermit who serves as Tristan's scribe when Tristan writes to Mark for clemency.

On the other hand, the heremetic return to the origins of the monastic spirit involved revolution, in both the root and the loose senses of that term: a return to *and* the overthrow of an origin. During his break with orthodox monasticism, Robert D'Arbrissel accused religious men of all ecclesiastical states (*doctores, episcopi et abbates et sacerdotes*) of being blunderers, liars, adulterers, slanderers, practitioners of incest, and of being ignorant and without charity. Yet such revolutions quickly led to even more radical subversion. The independence of hermits allowed them to wander, to preach, and to gather alms—above all in the city from which they were supposedly refugees (Génicot, p. 60). As opposed to their cloistered brothers, wandering hermits were also free to exchange ideas, inciting even charges of heresy. (It is no accident that the Franciscan order would be summoned into existence by a Vatican eager to purify and control the radical thrust of hermitism as it was affecting urban intellectuals.) Moreover, the image of the true hermit engendered the image (or the reality) of false hermitage as well, as evidenced by the poem of Payen Bolotin, written in the 1130s, which claims to excoriate a new social pestilence composed of radicals dressing as hermits, begging for alms, and living as vagagonds, parasites, lechers, hypocrites, and so on.[34] The hermit is therefore also an image, in twelfth century culture, of both radical withdrawal into an extreme monastic isolation and radical openness which tends toward subversion of the most scandalous sort, one that threatens not only the institution of monasticism, but also the metaphysical discourse which is its foundation.

We find in the historical case of Abelard an example that illustrates the contradictory resonances, both ideological and metaphysical, surrounding the eremitical impulse, and an example that, for Chrétien, was surely very close to home. In 1122, following his demystification of the supposed origins of the Abbey of St. Denis, Abelard escaped to Champagne, where Suger and the bishop allowed him to build a hermitage with a mud-and-straw oratory on some land outside of Troyes given to him by Thibaud de Champagne.[35] Abelard was followed there by a band of students of logic, who tilled the ground and rebuilt the oratory, which they named the "Paraclete," to the scandal of religious custom. Not surprisingly, it was St. Bernard, Abbot of Clairvaux, who apparently led the ensuing campaign against Abelard, successfully forcing his departure to another monastery (St. Gildas de Ruys) where Abelard became, himself, abbot during a short but stormy period.

Thus, Chrétien's hermit illustrates, by his apparently contradictory life styles, contrary perspectives upon the hermitage movement as it was seen in Chrétien's own time. There are other cultural questions, as well, raised by Chrétien's depicting the spontaneous rise (or regeneration) of commerce in a sylvan hermitage. If the church, until Chrétien's time, had been the principal custodian of literacy (many have supposed that Chrétien himself was at least in minor orders), the hermit, seen as a prototype of the ideal, charitable merchant, may also be seen as the emblem of a new kind of literacy, one that was doctrinally independent, open, errant, and polemical. Moreover, surely the mercantile class of Chrétien's own milieu was now arrogating for itself the power of literacy as an instrument indispensable to the new and more sophisticated techniques of international commerce. I have already underscored a basic homology between the chivalric hero and the *litteratus*, and I would suggest that Chrétien is now extending his model-making in order to expand with the hermit what we may call, using Brian Stock's term, a new "textual community" whose members include merchants, their aristocratic patrons, and certain revolutionary ecclesiastical figures emblematized by the hermit. We recall that Hugh of St. Victor says that the god of merchants is Mercury, god of rhetoric, who was also for the Greeks, Hermes, and for the Egyptians, Toth, inventor of writing (*Didascalicon* 2.24). The idea that the hermit would enlist his intellectual powers not only in the service of the spiritual commerce of souls in the economy of salvation, but also in the horizontal transactions of a more mercantile sort implies a both a new combination of values and a new kind of eloquence that reflects profound mutations in the discursive configurations of twelfth-century culture. For if Hugh of St. Victor can say of commerce, "This art is beyond all doubt a peculiar sort of rhetoric — strictly of its own kind — for eloquence is in the highest degree necessary to it," then it is not difficult to see how the model of commercial eloquence, which is by definition competitive and polemical (though not polemical in the manner of knights) might be linked with the movement of radical hermitage in a single "textual community." For it was precisely as itinerant, begging preachers began to circulate among urban crowds that many traditional doctrines began to be challenged in the free exchange of ideas. Did Chrétien see his own literacy, which was obviously in some sense up for hire to such wealthy patrons of commerce as Henri-le-libéral and Philippe de Flandres, as "Mercurial," that is, as both spiritual and mercantile?[36]

Since we do not know who Chrétien was, we cannot answer such a question. However, it would seem that medieval romance called from within for a more ample figure to emblematize the ambivalence of its own textuality, and that figure was Merlin. Indeed, Merlin is an amazing accretion of contradictory functions, many of which are anticipated here in Chrétien's rather cautious fiction of Yvain's meeting with the hermit in Broceliande. Howard Bloch has recently explored Merlin's functions as an emblem of writing:

> In classical mythology the invention of writing is variously ascribed to the Phoenician Cadmus, the Greek Hermes, or the Egyptian Thoth. The medieval figures are Odin, the inventor of runes, and Merlin — magician, enchanter and prophet. Merlin is said to have introduced writing to the Arthurian world and to have formulated plans for two books, each possessing its own discourse, logic, and epistemological mode.[37]

These two books, as Bloch characterizes them, implicate, first, a model built on the claim of origins, even though this book of the past is the "Devil's terrain"; and second, a book without origins that is "a spontaneously generated, autonomous discourse cut off from discernible origins. The book without origins is an original book: nonrepresentational, beholden to nothing, always true because consistently self-referential. Since it lies beyond any system of meaning outside of itself, its self-generating and self-determining language is situated beyond the limits of truth and falsehood" (p. 128). Although Bloch does not say so, we may see in these two opposed functions of writing an interesting analogy with the poetics of the *chanson de geste* (as exemplified by the first part of the *Roland*) as opposed to the poetics of romance (as exemplifed by *Yvain*). In other words, it is possible to find in the overlapping textuality of dissident hermits and of merchants manifestations of a new cultural ambivalence toward the power of writing expressed by romance authors diegetically in the figure of Merlin, if we may accept Bloch's account of him:

> The medieval Merlin is a polysemous figure. Representative of Satan, recuperated by God, he retains the knowledge imparted by both. A fatherless being without discernible origin, his conception having oc-

curred without his mother's awareness, he is at the same time the guardian of paternity. Merlin's function is bound to the discovery and relation of false and elusive family bonds, illegitimacy and incest as well as the genealogy of generations to come. A medieval Hermes, Merlin is the inhabitant of the forest, the Wild Man who is simultaneously the bringer of culture, the master of arts and of science. In Geoffrey of Monmouth's *Vita Merlini* he is, like Hermes, the practitioner of music, astronomy, mathematics, and calculation; he is particularly adept at keeping the written records of gestation which afford this fatherless guardian of letters a perfect perception of lineal relations. Also like Hermes – the god of clever speech, the wise child, the flatterer and liar, Merlin repesents the skillful rhetorician and master of juridical discourse. (p. 129)

It is no doubt pertinent to recall here that *Yvain* was written precisely at the time when, according to Jacques Le Goff, a new theology of Purgatory was constituting itself in European culture and specifically in intellectual milieux in which Chrétien himself was versed, namely, those of Cîteaux and Paris.[38] This new doctrine involved the belief that the purgation of sins after death occurred in a specific place beyond the material world where the souls of sinners spent limited periods of time until, once purified by torture and hardship, they were pardoned for their sins and saved in Heaven. It was a place of just prices where time had quantity and value and where distances to be traversed by penitent souls were precise (Le Goff, pp. 310–11). If it is safe to say that courtly erotic discourse drew heavily for its *matière* upon conventions of mystical discourse, it is likely that there was also feedback and that an economy of wordly desire conceptually perfected in a vernacular poetics worked major mutations in mystical and metaphysical discourse: such intercontamination of codes, I would suggest, was one consequence of vernacularizing *grammatica* in a culture where commerce was on the rise. In other words, courtly erotic discourse did not deconstruct the metaphysical, but altered it from below.

Given that the forest, in Chrétien's system of values is a locus of openness, Haidu's modern concept of the hermitage as a rural "closed" economy is dissonant. Also dissonant is his idea that the economy of the city is "open" and that it "deconstructs" the "closed" any more than human deconstructs animal, reason deconstructs passion, or city deconstructs forest. Rather, we should consider Chrétien's textual poesis as integral to a much broader ideological enterprise, one in which the closure of systems (textual, monetary, logical, judicial) is seen as the possibility of bringing the multiple into the corporate, the confused into the distinct, and the stochastic into the regular and of making the warrior into the domesticated spouse and breeder. It is through closures of form, measure, and economy that desiring Nature succeeds herself without dying, and it is through form that God and poets alike "exornate" the *materia* of raw nature

(vegetable, animal, human) in order to bring to it the perfection or complete-
ness, both cosmic and esthetic, that it craves. Such is Chrétien's mandate as a
litteratus: to construct, out of the multiple codes competing with each other to
determine reality within his culture, a significant and sumptuous edifice in which
men and women could hope to live, if only in their imaginations.

Grammatica, in this sense, is not the Derridean *écriture* as many people, including Haidu, construe it. It is important for medievalists to understand that
écriture and "deconstruction" presuppose positive gestures that Derrida himself
considers as *con*structive. Asked recently whether critics should not be as receptive to texts attempting to *posit* closed significant structures, as they are to texts
that fail, contest, or betray the hidden metaphysics subtending most textual operations, beginning with the writing even of a complete sentence (*oratio perfecta*),
Derrida quickly answered that already in Heidegger, the terms *Destruktion* and
Abbau are not to be understood simply as "destruction," but rather as the attempt
to "défaire une édification pour voir comment elle est constituée ou déconstituée"
("to take apart an edifice to see how it is constituted or unconstituted"). As for
a "schéma de la déconstruction qui serait celui d'une opération technique s'appli-
quant à démonter des systèmes, personnellement je ne souscris pas à ce modèle
de la déconstruction" ("schema of deconstruction which might be that of a technical operation applied to taking apart systems, I personally do not subscribe to
that model of deconstruction"), Derrida says that the true object of deconstruction is not "structure" in the sense that structuralists of the sixties gave to that
term, but rather, classical ontology in a philosophical tradition:

> "Quand d'autres s'y sont intéressés, j'ai essayé de le déterminer, ce
> concept, à ma manière; enfin selon ce que je croyais être la bonne
> manière, c'est-à-dire en insistant sur le fait qu'il ne s'agissait pas d'une
> opération négative. Je ne me sens pas en situation de choisir entre une
> opération disons négative, nihiliste, qui viendrait s'acharner pour
> démonter des systèmes et l'autre opération. J'aime beaucoup tout ce
> que je déconstruis à ma manière."[39]

> When others became interested in it, I tried to determine this concept
> in my own way — finally, in what I thought to be the correct way — that
> is, by insisting on the fact that it was not a negative operation. I do
> not feel that I am in a situation to choose between an operation that
> we might call negative or nihilistic, bent upon taking apart systems, or
> the other operation. I very much love what I deconstruct in my own
> way.

For Chrétien, the city and the economics of the city are not *openings* of what
was *rurally* closed, but rather the opposite, and like his patrons, he saw such
closures as postive and life-giving, not alienating. The vocabulary of a Marxist
semiotic reading of *Yvain* may very well convey meaning to a critic previously

aligned to a certain historical schema that sees early capitalism and nascent urbanism as alienating, however such a schema seems facile to me, at least to the
extent that it ignores the massive and irreversible regrouping in twelfth-century
urban life of human energies and allegiances in ways that were also liberating,
by any scale of values. We shall return to the notion of closure as both an ethical
and an artistic value at the end of the following chapter.

Chapter 6
From Man-Beast to Lion-Knight: Difference, Kind, and Emblem

Chrétien's understanding of *conjointure* as the potential—not merely to drama-tize unstated relationships between objects, circumstances, or episodes in his narrative, but to conceive his *matière* topically—meant that he could understand narrative relationships abstractly: as "places" that are "empty" because they can subsist in the intellect independently of the specific content that can "fill" them. The abstractness of topical *conjointure*, understood as the primary condition of truth in narrative, made it possible for Chrétien to refract the single, topically conceived relationship between a "special" man and his generic animality through many different circumstantial perspectives, and also to invoke multiple types of signs and discursive strategies in order to convey this relationship.

Thus, the progress of Yvain from bestiality in the forest to his restored mar-riage with Laudine and to the social world as a rehabilitated, courteous knight is articulated by Chrétien with the aid of a remarkable variety of narrative resources, thanks to which we are brought to understand the relationship of a man to his animal nature with as fully amplified a vision as possible. The last half of *Yvain* may be understood as a transition from a man as pure, undifferen-tiated animal to the "different" perfection of animality in a loving and courteous knight.

In other words, the stable topical armature of Chrétien's narrative makes pos-sible a striking dynamism in his poetic invention: symbols become movable, act-ing as "shifters" between different systems and discourses (the psychic, the so-cial, the religious), and symbols are artfully substituted for each other in the narrative chain without a loss of *sens*, or coherence. This dynamism in Chrétien's construing of narrative content presupposed a new sense of freedom, nurtured by logic, of his art from the claims of ontological truth (though not from those of formal truth), and hastened a mature understanding of narrative as fiction that is *about* reality yet distinct *from* it because such art is both a product and an object of the intellect. Chrétien's success in exploiting the polyvalence of narrative substance in order to inculcate in his stories an internal life of their own may be seen as a positive poetic response to the tragic slippage and vitiation of signs that marked the internal process of the *Roland*. Let us now explore these propositions in more detail.

One day as Yvain sleeps "poor and naked" ("*povre et nu*," l. 2912) in the forest, that is, hovering on a very fine line between the animal and vegetable states[1] (he can sink no lower), some noble maidens happen to pass by and recognize Yvain, even in his degraded state, by a scar on his face. To the extent that this scar is, quite literally, the inscription of previous feats of arms on his flesh, hence, of a certain heroic value, this inscription determines and signifies, within the discourse of a specific social group, his original noble and chivalric "character," in the original Greek sense of that term. A character, Mark Shell reminds us, is "the upper die used by the coinmaker or impressed mark upon the coin."[2] Yvain's pale and naked body is a kind of hieroglyphic text, a caroglyph pitifully inferior to the heroic text of Roland's body fixed in its monumental posture of defiance even in death: is not Charlemagne, in this sense, the first reader of the *Chanson de Roland?* Diligent readers of scars on chivalric flesh that they are, the noble maidens read Yvain's story by a different, less epic heroic code and rush back to their unmarried mistress, the Dame de Noroison, to tell their story of having seen the "most proven and the best furnished knight in the world" ("*Le chevalier miauz esprové / Del monde et le maiuz antechié*," ll. 2922–23). Since Yvain is naked, the nature of his "furnishings" is hardly ambiguous. The new code of romance is working well. The Dame de Noroison promptly orders the maidens to return to annoint the naked hero with a magic unguent. In Hugh of St. Victor's scheme of the seven mechanical arts, Yvain will now benefit from the sixth, which is medicine. So enthusiastic are the maidens with their task, however, that, instead of rubbing only Yvain's temples, as their mistress had commanded, they rub Yvain's body from head to toe, whereupon Yvain is suddenly resurrected from near vegetativeness to his elementary, but proper (though still naked), state of *homo erectus*. The damsels will be rewarded, and not punished, for their *démesure* in applying five full *cestiers* of the marvelous unguent to his body — that is, about ten gallons by the old Parisian measurement of liquid *sétiers*. First, though, the maidens give Yvain clothes (the fruit of humanity's first mechanical skill, weaving), and then they bring him to the Dame de Noroison's castle. Here Yvain is thoroughly redomesticated by being bathed, coiffed, and shaven, hence, by being shorn of the uncouth iconography of the traditional wild man of medieval legend that he had previously displayed.

Yvain's good fortune here reflects the earlier laundering of his unsavory past undertaken by Lunette (another just measurer of the exchange value of knights) when she first presented Yvain to the widow of the man he had just slain. Chrétien clearly expects us to weigh Yvain's forthcoming merits in serving the Dame de Noroison not only contextually with regard to what he owes her for rescuing him, but also more abstractly, with regard to Laudine, in whose eyes Yvain's credit has vanished. Thus, when Yvain is at last armed with fine weapons and a horse (signalling once again his ascension to the arts of weaponry and knighthood), the damsels' earlier *démesure* with the ointment is now repaid by equivalent exploits on the battlefield as Yvain protects the Dame de Noroison from the assault of hostile neighbors, just as, earlier, he had protected Laudine.

However, we of the audience witness the carnage that Yvain inflicts upon his enemy not through the eyes of the narrator, but through those of the unmarried Dame and her maidens: not only do they exclaim that Roland himself could never have achieved with his sword Durendal what Yvain is achieving now, but also they make it clear that the violence of this hero's sword in battle summons to their minds the contrary *gestes* of that other, less bellicose skirmish in which Enide proved her sweet prowess on her wedding night:

> Et dient que buer seroit née
> Cui il avroit s'amor donée
> Que si est as armes puissanz.
> (ll. 3243–45)

And they say that she to whom he might give his love—he who is so powerful at arms—she would be born to a happy fate.

Here is a crucial moment where Chrétien refracts hyperbolic male heroism (and male narrativity) through female eyes, allowing us to glimpse, through these lovely prisms, the polysemy of epic heroic motivation. The Dame de Noroison's hyperbole not only eroticizes the chivalric battlefield, but also proclaims a superiority of Yvain over Roland that is both qualitative *and* quantitative: the new hero of romance is stronger than the best hero of epic; he also manifests a new and radical dynamism of soul that the hero of the older code could never have honorably displayed.[3] The *Roland* poet never tells us when or if Roland ever changes his clothes: armor alone maketh the man. Yvain, by contrast, like Calogrenant and other heroes of Chrétien's romances, bathes and changes from armor to luxurious robes whenever—and well before—the prospect of female companionship presents itself. To put it more bluntly, Yvain's value as marrying and breeding stock now matches and even subsumes his valor of the sword, even though good knights (as Laudine has learned) are not so easily domesticated.

Admirable though Yvain's rehabiliation is, both as a potential lover and as a knight, his spectacular protection of the Dame de Noroison's domain is clearly only the first step in a rigorous economy of redemption which demands, on the part of the poem's audience, an active perception of equivalences, and this entails special alertness to Chrétien's own symbol-making process. Thus, precisely as Yvain takes up his quest for redeemed (and redeemable) honor, Chrétien "finds" in his story a new emblem for Yvain's animal nature: this lion, whom Yvain "loves like his own body" (*"l'aime come mon cors,"* l. 3798) also happens to be the king of beasts, a symbol of the resurrected Christ, and a creature variously celebrated by the bestiaries not just for its ferocity, but also for its compassion, temperance, watchfulness, tameability, loyalty, and monogamy as well. Topically speaking, if Yvain is a human, he is an animal; now, *ethically* speaking, he is no longer just *any* animal: by metonymy he is now associated with leoninity, a positive association that will be amplified by the story.

Such a comparison had been partially prepared by various similes appearing earlier in Chrétien's own tale. Esclados, Yvain's predecessor in marriage with Laudine, had been compared to a raging lion when he attacked Calogrenant (l. 488), and Yvain himself had seemed lionlike during his ferocious defense of the Dame de Noroison:

> Tot autressi antr'aus se fiert
> Con li lions antre les dains,
> Quant l'angoisse et chace la fains.
> (ll. 3202–4)

He rages among them like a lion among deer, when he is driven by the anguish of hunger.

This earlier image has cultural resonances that are already complex. On the one hand, it brings descriptive vividness to a battle scene in which the explicit comparison of Yvain to Roland is reinforced by a metaphor common to both poems:

> Quant Rolland veit que la bataille serat,
> Plus se fait fiers que leon ne leupart.
> (ll. 1110–11)

When Roland sees that battle will occur, he becomes fiercer than a lion or a leopard.

On the other hand, the details of Chrétien's image are much closer to those of Virgil's *Aeneid*, where the pejorative bestiality of warriors transported by unheroic rage reaches a terrifying crescendo in the second half of that poem. Here is Virgil's more expansive simile describing Mezzentius, king of the Etruscans:

> Impastus stabula alta leo ceu saepe peragrans
> (suadet enim vesana fames), si forte fugacem
> conspexit capream aut surgentem in cornua cervum,

gaudet hians immane comasque arrexit et haeret
visceribus super accumbens—lavit improba
taeter ora cruor—
sic ruit in densos alacer Mezentius hostis.

(10. 723–29)

Just as a ravenous lion who often goes ranging
  through deep forest coverts, while
Hunger makes him more fierce, perhaps sights a bounding
  she-goat
Or a stag towering to his antlers, rejoices and opens
Wide his huge mouth, his mane bristling up as he crouches,
Clinging upon the beast's entrails as hideous gore
Bathes his cruel jaws,
Thus eager Mezzentius attacked his close-ranked opponents.[4]

Given that metaphors are speech acts that always signify *discursively*, and not
in isolation, Chrétien has "found" in the lion a symbol whose polyvalence will
mark his text as a shifter between multiple discourses (Biblical, classical,
folkoric, "scientific"),[5] all of which he entertains, yet controls, as he distributes
them within the economy of his own story, thereby asserting the preeminence
of his *own* poetic voice as a vernacular *litteratus* over the tangled legacy of discourses inherent in his *matière*.

Animalities and Models of Perception

From our very first perception of the *lion* as he struggles in the forest with the
serpent, it is clear that we are invited, along with Yvain, to "think" the lion's
animality not only as an isolated symbol, but also in a differential *system* constituted by multiple animalities pertinent to Yvain's own, as a man. Moreover,
to "think" animality in the context of twelfth-century culture involved distinctly
different hermeneutical alternatives: the moral or allegorical, the rational or
"scientific," and what I shall later call the "heraldic" or "totemic." I shall propose,
first, that Chrétien's poem entertains, at different moments, all of these alternatives, and second, that the *interplay* between these different cognitive procedures
evinced by Chrétien's *Yvain* constitutes a basic intellectual game that is still possible for us to play today to the extent that, even now, we still tend to perceive
animals in our culture with analogous, if not always identical, teleologies in
mind.

When Yvain sees the lion and the serpent deadlocked in mortal combat, with
the serpent clinging to the lion's tale, a choice based on *judgment* becomes necessary: which of the animals—the lion, the serpent, or even Yvain himself—

deserves the most consideration in Yvain's course of action? The process of judgment defines the moral state of Yvain himself in his role as judge: to choose lioninity over serpentinity is a moral choice of good over evil. To save the lion at the subsequent risk of his own well-being is to indicate, further, that Yvain is motivated by the passion of charity rather than by cupidity, as he apparently was before.

The moral or allegorical classification of animals had of course been dominant in neoplatonic and Augustinian exegetical traditions of medieval culture, and these criteria certainly still pertain to our perception of both the lion and the serpent. However, in Chrétien's culture, such tendencies to construe mythical archetypes in vernacular poetry were nourished not only by Scripture, but also by classical letters, and even by folklore, and such hybridized symbols were already current in the bestiaries of Chrétien's own time. That Chrétien drew heavily upon the classical and Scriptural traditions (whether directly or through bestiaries) is obvious, and it is possible (as Julian Harris did so well in 1948) to construct a cogent reading of the lion's symbolic functions in *Yvain* based above all on the multiple, but concordant, virtues of the lion as an allegorical and fabulous beast. Thus, the lion embodies, in Chrétien's story, not only the congenial features celebrated in him by the bestiaries or by the story of Androcles, but also a theological dimension of divine grace which is shown in this story to be at work even in the remotest corners of the world.[6]

However, there was another classical and medieval tradition of classifying animals which was not fabulous or allegorical, but rational and "scientific," at least in the medieval sense of that term. Such rationalism was once again gaining prominence in Chrétien's culture with the rise of Aristotelianism, known both directly (as in the case of texts such as the *Categories* and the *Topics*, which were known in the twelfth century) and indirectly (as in Porphyry's and Boethius's readings of such Aristotelian texts). In this tradition, criteria of classification were not moral, but ontological, and they led to the systematic construing of differences (*differentiae*) perceived by the mind in such a way as to divide *genera* properly into their various species and to define what features constitute this or that species.

In logical terms, a species is defined by medieval logicians as a genus plus a *differentia*: thus, the species "human" is the genus "animal" plus the *differentia* "rational." Some *differentiae* are separable from a given species (e.g., two-footedness), and some are *in*separable (e.g., to be capable of laughing, or *risibilis*). Porphyry the Phoenician, whose *Isagoge* (translated into Latin by Boethius) became one of the most important resources of twelfth-century logic, speaks thus of the relationships possible between species and *differentiae*:

There are separable and inseparable differences. Moving, resting, being healthy, being ill, and characteristics similar to those are separable, but being hook-nosed, snub-nosed, rational, or irrational are inseparable. Some inseparable differences exist *per se*, some accidentally. Rational, mortal, and being capable of knowledge belong to man *per se*, but hooknoosed or snub-nosed belong accidentally and not *per se*. Differences present *per se*, then, are comprehended in the definition of the substance and make another essence, but accidental differences are not comprehended in the definition of the substance and do not make another essence but only a difference in quality.[7]

In her excellent discussion of *differentiae* in Porphyry, Eleonore Stump writes:

Differentiae can be thought of in two different ways: either they divide a genus, in which case they are divisive differentiae; or they constitute a species, in which case they are constitutive differentiae. The same differentia is both divisive and constitutive, but it is divisive of one thing and constitutive of another. For example, the differentia *rational* is divisive of the genus animal and constitutive of the species man. A genus that cannot itself be subsumed as a species under some higher genus is called a highest genus—Aristotle's ten categories are the ten highest genera of everything; and a species that can have no species subsumed under it for which it serves as a genus is called a lowest species. Except for lowest species and highest genera, all genera are subaltern genera—that is, they can be described also as species; and all species are subaltern species—that is, they can all be described as genera.[8]

Such epistemic operations tend to give rise to a characteristic cognitive paradigm, which is a tree, and the "Porphyrian tree" became, through Abelard, a constitutive model of twelfth-century scholastic thought. For example, if we may think of substance as a genus that is not a species of anything and hence is a highest genus, let us see how the Porphyrian tree of differences "works" when we think "human" as—opposed, for example, to "God" (see schema, page 87).

We should be reassured, however, that the both Porphyry and the scholastics knew that their cognitive processes were not really as formally determined by treeness as it might appear. Umberto Eco has recently shown how, from Porphyry on, the model of the tree always turns into an epistemological hindrance when it is discovered that

(a) the same differentia can encompass many species, (b) the same couple of differentiae can occur under more than one genus, (c) different couples of genera can be represented under many genera by using the same names (equivocally of analogically), and (d) it is an open question how high in the tree the common genus can be in respect to which many *subordinate* genera can host the same differentiae.[9]

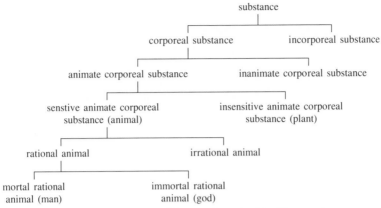

Reprinted from *Boethius's "De topicis differentiis,"* translated by Eleanore Stump.
Copyright © 1978 by Eleanore Stump. Used by permission of the publisher, Cornell
University Press.

Commenting upon Porphyry's comparison between the tree as a metaphor to describe relationships between individual, genus, and species and the family
"tree," Abelard concedes that the former teaches us to ascend from one clas-
sificatory step to another; but it is also a hindrance, he says, because in logic
we do not ascend (as we always do in the case of families) to a single origin (*ad
unum principium*).[10] The Porphyrean tree is not, in other words, a fixed or stable
model of being, but only a heuristic schema of cognition which allows us to construe terms and reason properly. Eco shows how the epistemic model of the tree
tends to collapse, when its heuristic limits have been reached, into the model of
the labyrinth: "The utopia of a Porphyrean tree represented the most influential
attempt to reduce the labyrinth into a bidimensional tree. But the tree again
generated the labyrinth" (p. 80).

Twelfth-century thought oscillated, however, between more than two hermeneutical paradigms. Indeed, there was an important third one that Eco (speaking not of of the twelfth century, but of Vico) calls the "heap." The "heap" is
characteristic of mystical human understanding of divine discourse: "The language of the gods is a heap of unrelated synechdoches and metonymies: thirty
thousand gods as identified by Varro, as many as the Greeks counted, including
stones, fountains, reefs, brooks, minute objects, signifiers of forces, causes,
connections" (p. 108). Perhaps I could suggest that in twelfth- and thirteenth-
century romance, a scientific tree of rational thought competes with the labyrinth
embodied in the experience of the quest, while the allegorical mode of romance
tends toward the heap, that is, toward the accumulation of multiple and disparate
significations where no perceptible criterion of combination exists. In romance,
the labyrinth and the heap tend to generate effects of the marvelous, understood
as the transgression of "treeness." In the *avanture* of romance, we are not al-

lowed to see the tree for the forest. With regard to *Yvain*, the bestiary serves
as an important heap of notions combined into a whimsical and eclectic amalgam
where *differentiae* of human and animal are construed in a tangle of anthropo-
morphic bestalities. Yvain's lion, whom the knight chances upon in the middle
of the forest, is a case in point: here is a creature whose impossible polysemy
is a ragbag of *differentiae* drawn from the core of the bestiary tradition. *Differen-*
tiae are conspicuously misplaced as this massively humanized *lion au chevalier*
becomes a symbol of Yvain's redeemed and noble animal nature as the *chevalier*
au lion. Thus, if we are told by the bestiary that the lion is faithful, forbearing,
compassionate, watchful, and abstemious, all of these positive ethical virtues are
illustrated by the lion's conduct in such a way as to stress his function as an in-
alienable symbol of Yvain's own animal nature, now properly domesticated by
reason.[11] As Chrétien says of the lion, "Forever more he will always accompany
him; he wishes to serve and protect him" (*"Toz jors mes ne s'an partira: / Que*
servir et garder le viaut." ll. 3413-15). When the lion smells game in the forest,
he awaits his master's command before killing the game; then, despite his hunger, the lion stoically lies motionless until he is at last permitted to devour the
remains of the deer's carcass in proper lionlike fashion, bones and all. This episode stands in clear contrast with the simile of the lion beserk with hunger with
which Chrétien had earlier described Yvain himself. Yvain, for his part, carefully skins and cuts up the quarry, showing his mastery of the mechanical and
very human art of *venatio*, once again in contrast, first, with the impulsive man-
beast at the beginning of the romance, who wore skins freshly torn from his
animals and, second, in contrast with his own conduct when he hunted and ate
raw game during his period of insanity in the forest before meeting the hermit.
This humble culinary moment in the forest joins reasonable human to passionate
beast in a duly harmonious relationship, even though Chrétien maintains a careful distinction between this still primitive meal in the forest and a truly civilized
meal of the court, since it does not yet include bread, wine, salt, or any of the
accoutrements or other "side dishes" of the courtly feast;

> Et met an une broche an rost
> Son lardé cuire au feu mout tost,
> S'el rosti tant que toz fu cuiz.
> Mais del mangier fu nus deduiz;
> Qu'il n'i out pain ne vin ne sel,
> Ne nape ne coutel ne el.
>
> (ll. 3465-70)

And he quickly puts his meat on a roasting spit and cooks it until it is
done; but he took no delight in the meal, since there was neither bread
nor wine, nor salt, nor tablecloth, nor knife, nor anything else.

Not being a banquet or feast, this silvan meal shared by a man and a lion obviously does not belong to the mechanical art called the "science of entertainments" (*scientia ludorum*): this is the last of the seven that Hugh of St. Victor mentions, and it includes banquets with songs, instrumental music, and chants.

Chrétien selects features of the bestiary lion which stress the restored subservience of animal to human, of passion to reason, virtues which of course reflect victories within his master's own soul. However, Chrétien is also careful to set natural limits to such subservience. Even in the bestiary we are told that "so far as their relations with men are concerned, the nature of lions is that they do not get angry unless they are wounded" (p. 9). In conformity with this limit, Chrétien constructs a sequence of three scenes (the fight with Harpin de la Montagne, the defense of Lunette, and the liberation of the enslaved maidens in the Chateau de Pesme Avanture in which the lion is thoughtlessly ordered by his master to stay by the sidelines while Yvain fights. Yvain's error here recalls that of Erec when he commands Enide to follow him in silence, no matter what happens. Like faithful Enide, each time the lion sees that his master is certain to be wounded or even slain, the lion spontaneously violates Yvain's orders and leaps to his rescue. Chrétien is warning us, in an unstoic (and unPauline) way, not to allow reason foolishly to legislate all passion from our being and to overdomesticate our animal will: a man must not deny, to the point of self-destruction, his generic nature as animal.

The lion's relationship to Yvain is both personal and symbolic, then, in that he not only adores his master but symbolizes his master's redeemed animal nature: *si homo bonus est, bonus animalis est*. Moreover, the lion's nature is *perfected* in that of his master, just as human nature as animal *and* human is perfected in the incarnate Christ, the immortal god who took the form — both spiritual and animal — of a mortal man in order to erase the tragic difference (both ontological and moral) between fallen man and fallen woman and their original created forms as they must have been beside the tree of knowledge.

An erasure of differential relationships between human and animal in *Yvain, ou le chevalier au lion* invites *pathos* when Yvain himself regresses into his generic animality in the forest. However, an uncanny *humor* arises the more Yvain's lion is humanized. What male reader does not wince when Yvain smites off the end of the lion's tale as he delivers him from the evil serpent? What reader, male or female, would not start if Yvain and his lion walked through the door into his home? Although the lion cannot speak, he is eloquent with conventional body signs: he kneels before Yain with his paws joined, like a good vassal during rites of hommage; he weeps abundant tears in gratitude for his rescue. The lion is courteous at supper, and he even shares the same bedroom with his master in the Castle of Noire Espine. It is also here that two maidens skilled in medicine treat the lion's wounds, exactly as maidens do, by convention, for a wounded knight. So embued is the lion with a classical sense of loyalty that when Yvain appears to have died during a faint, the lion sets his master's sword against a tree and prepares himself, like a good Roman, to run upon it. The lion is also clever, almost to the point of being rational: when Yvain shuts the lion in a room as he fights with the three sons of the demon in the Château de Pesme Avanture, the lion seeks a way of escape until he finds a rotten section of the doorsill, which he scratches until he can pass under the door and rescue his master, just in the nick of time.

However, such humor is perhaps "uncanny" in a special sense of that word, that is, as the English term to translate Freud's notion of the *Unheimliche*. Thanks to the rich lexical ambiguities of the German, the *Unheimliche* expresses that ambivalence provoked in the mind by things perceived as uncanny: such things, Freud says, threaten to reactivate experiences in our unconscious which have been repressed because they are dangerous to our being as social animals:

> If psychoanalytic theory is concrete in maintaining that every emotional affect, whatever its quality, is transformed by repression into morbid anxiety, then among such cases of anxiety there must be a class in which the anxiety can be shown to come from something repressed which recurs. This class of morbid anxiety would then be no other than what is uncanny, irrespective of whether it originally aroused dread or some other affect . . . if this is indeed the secret nature of the uncanny, we can understand why the usage of speech has extended *das Heimliche* into its opposite *das Unheimliche*; for this uncanny is in reality nothing new or foreign, but something familiar and old-established in the mind that has been estranged only by the process of repression.[12]

Si est homo, est animal: the lion is uncanny because we see in him the domestication of our own savage animality, and in this romance, such domestication involved a symbolic sacrifice similar to that of circumcision, hence, similar (like circumcision) to castration. Indeed, since Yvain has, in a sense, fornicated against Laudine by indulging his passion for chivalric glory, the loss of his animal's tale expresses a justice similar to that of Oedipus's blinding himself. As Freud writes, "In blinding himself, Oedipus, that mythical law-breaker, was simply carrying out a mitigated form of the punishment of castration — the only punishment that according to the *lex talionis* was fitted for him"). 383).

On the other hand, Chrétien is neither a Freudian, nor a Stoic, nor Augustinian neoplatonist. Nor is he a fanatic about repressing animal appetition in humans, whether anger or desire. Thus despite the heap-like aspect of its cognitive processes as expressed in the mode of the *avanture* in romance teems with multiple animalities (including, of course, those of lion and human whose web of relationships do finally express an "arboreal" architecture that is natural and true (in

Aristotelian terms), and is therefore in opposition with the *de*naturing figural tradition proper to Augustinian neoplatonism.

In other words, *Yvain, ou le chevalier au lion* makes more than one cognitive demand of its audience. On the one hand, it expresses many different animalities woven into its *matière*, whether through simile, through narrative event, or by "association" of function (for instance, as in the provision of fur, feathers, hides or food) into Chrétien's narrative text, and they include the following species: peacock, bull, horse, elephant, owl, cat, human, deer, chamois, stag, boar, bird, eagle dog, sparhawk, crane, chicken (as capon), ermine, lion, serpent, bear, and otter. On the other hand, this tapestry of animalities does finally express a network of different features and functions that corresponds to a a physical universe which is coherently structured and hierarchal, and not, therefore, inherently evil.

To the contrary, the lion serves as a corrective, not of human animal nature *per se*, but only of perversions of humans, whether as an animal who has been made foolishly weak by misguided reason, or as an animal who has turned its animal nature to unnatural, improper ends. Thus, the first adversary of Yvain's animal is the tyrannical and sexually perverse giant, Harpin de la Montagne, who has threatened to kill the four remaining sons of an aged knight unless he delivers his daughter to him, whom he will in turn give over to his vilest varlets as a prostitute (*a putage*, l. 4125). Although giants were not considered to belong to a different species of animal from humans (but as an anomaly of that species), giants were treated exactly like other monsters in medieval sermons and bestiaries and were moralized according to the same procedures. John Bloch Friedman writes:

> The medieval propensity for moralizing or drawing spiritual instruction from all aspects of the natural world is especially marked in homiletic treatments of the monstrous races. Certain medieval bestiaries interpolated among their animals a section of the Plinian races, and moralized them much as they moralized the pelican or the unicorn. Collections of exempla drew *moralitates* from the races, making them into figures for unattractive human qualities and vices.[13]

A connection between the giant Harpin's divergence from the norms of a man as a properly social species and his unnatural sexuality is not difficult to see. In contrast with the man-beast at the beginning of the romance, who symbolized the human appetitive self as seen by Calogrenant in a neutral perspective, Harpin is a symbol of monstrously unnatural appetition at work in society and is therefore the natural (and social) human's unnatural adversary. When Yvain begins to fight Harpin, he strikes Harpin in the chest, piercing the bearskin that the giant wears ("bear" is another emblem of wildness, according to the bestiaries), yet Yvain is not powerful enough to overcome the giant by himself. Perceiving his master's dilemma, the lion leaps unsollicited into the fray, and first tears the hairy skin (*"pel velue*," l. 4223) off the giant's flanks, and then tears a great hunk of flesh from his thighs, whereupon the giant roars and cries out like a mad bull. Given the motif of sexual perversion in this episode, it would be difficult not to see this mutilation as another well-merited symbolic castration. However, it is not a man's animal nature *per se* that is being punished here, but rather, willful perversions of a man's animality. In short, the lion is acting in this episode as a positive force of nature which must defy denaturing repression. If the giant is to be understood as an extreme figuration of Yvain's own erring disposition, may we not, with hindsight, see his excessive tourneying as another form of "gigantic" *putage?*

In the Chateau de Pesme Avanture episode we find an even more penetrating revindication of man's and woman's animal nature as a force that must not be unduly repressed at the expense of his or her vital needs. This time the force of repression to be overcome is that fetishizing impulse where the love of money and of fine objects (including even romances) subverts proper bonds of reciprocity (among them, courtesy and the custom of aristocratic hospitality) within the feudal structure and which, in Chrétien's eyes, is therefore unnatural. As international trade began to transform social and economic relationships in his world, Chrétien remained eager to expose the social abuses that it encouraged, though to do so in a way that was congruous with the social values and idiom of his aristocratic patrons. In this scene, Yvain's triumph will be to deliver three hundred maidens who weave silk (and not wool, as do less aristocratic workers in Flanders, just to the west of Champagne) in an atelier which exploits them ruthlessly: we are being clearly told that the profit motive can incite humans to drive their fellow humans into bestiality. Since the production of silk was not indigenous to Northern France, the Château de Pesme Avanture perhaps connotes social practices of a marvelous "realism" which, Chrétien is telling us, must not be allowed to flourish in Champagne. Imprisoned as slaves, and even as animals, the maidens produce exquisite silk fabric, we are told, but they do so at the expense of their own physical well-being, including, of course, their natural beauty:

> "Toz jours dras de soie tistrons,
> Ne ja n'an serons miauz vestues.
> Toz jors serons povres et nues
> Et toz jors fain et soif avrons;
> Ja tant gaeignier ne savrons,
> Que miauz an aliiens a mangier.
> Del pain avons a grant dangier,
> Au main petit et au soir mains
> Que ja de l'uevre de noz mains

N'avra chascune por son vivre
Que quatre deniers de la livre."
(ll. 5298–5308)

"All of our days we shall weave silk, yet we shall never be better
clothed because of it. All our days we shall be poor and naked, and
all of our days we shall be hungry and thirsty. Nor will we earn
enough to eat any better. We are very short of bread: we have little in
the morning, and less in the evening. For the work of our hands each
of us will earn but four pence of a pound."

The adversaries whom Yvain must fight in order to deliver these maidens are
not ordinary members of the human species, but are born of a woman and a
devil. Moreover, they are not a single, noble adversary, but doubles of each
other, basely born of an unnatural copulation. As unnatural doubles, they are
perhaps symbols of profit begotten usuriously: usury, it was argued, is money
begotten unnaturally of money, nothing of nothing, at the expense of both logic
and of natural laws. It is in the character of art composed for a twelfth-century
aristocratic patron, whose status was now based on the privilege of lineage, to
portray social abuses as consequences of genealogical errors, especially incest.
Indeed, the family "tree" became, in Chrétien's world, an important foundation
for the "truth" of aristocratic authority. As R. Howard Bloch writes:

With the fixation of the noble family on its own soil came a certain
narrowing of its peripheral limits and a reorientation of its conceptual
base—from the spatialized "horizontal" clan to the more vertically and
temporally conceived lineage. This process represented more than a
mere institutional shift; it implied, in fact, an important "prise de con-
science" on the part of the aristocratic kin group of the necessity for
biopolitical management of its own resources, both human and material. More precisely, it involved: restriction and control of marriage in
consonance with social, military, and economic interests; adoption of a
system of succession that assured the integral transmission of family
holdings; abd certain awareness of a specifically aristocratic mode of
wealth, real property (*proprietas*), which is connatural—both historically and ideologically—with the primogenital articulation of lineage
itself.[14]

In the Château de Pesme Avanture, we witness not only the unjust repression
of humans' physical well-being for the sake of profit, but the decline or abuse
of many of the seven mechanical arts: weaving, weaponry (the devil's sons fight
with clubs against Yvain's chivalric arms), medicine, commerce, "venery," and
even theatrics, the *scientia ludorum*, if we may see the bad hospitality and the
scene in the garden as perversions of the natural end of the courtly social world,

which is the feast where adventures are told before an assembly of knights and ladies. We will recall that in this garden a very beautiful sixteen-year-old maiden reads an anonymous romance (*"ne sai de cui,"* l. 5366) to her father and the rest of the family, who recline on a rug of silk (*"qui se gisoit / Sor un drap de soie,"* ll. 5363–64) presumably produced by the enslaved young maidens of the same household. Chrétien is apparently introducing, here, a thinly coded complaint against those in power (perhaps, even, the Counts of Champagne) who now patronized the exploitive production not only of textiles, but also of texts as well: that is, the production of romances as consumer items by underpaid, writing workers of the vernacular chancery (presumably such as Chrétien) who could well have viewed the reading of their anonymous romances by ravishing maidens in gardens as a kind of castration. It is perhaps worth noting that Chrétien wrote *Le conte del graal* in the Court of Flanders, where he praised Philippe's generosity with special emphasis.

Just as certain leaders of feudal society tolerate the unjust claustration of workers, so too Yvain unwisely consents to shut his lion in a room before undertaking his combat with the devil's sons. Since Yvain is unequivocally foolish for agreeing to such terms, clearly the lion is wise in breaking out of his sequestration, despite Yvain's wishes, in order to save his master — and, by extension, to rescue the enthralled workers. If Yvain and his lion, together, serve in this episode as a messianic symbol, as some have argued, then the same topical truth "from species" pertains here as elsewhere: if Christ is a man, he is an animal. Nor is such a proposition degrading: to the contrary, the inconography of Christ underwent an interesting transformation in Chrétien's time: the stern, resurrected Christ sitting in judgment now tended to give way to the crucified, suffering, human Christ with whom natural, "passional" man and woman could readily identify without declaring war on their own worldly, animal nature.

From Social Differences to the Totemic Text

Earlier in this chapter, I mentioned, among the various modes of "thinking" animality, what I called the "heraldic," or, in more modern terms, the "totemic," and I shall close with some brief remarks about heraldic or totemic emblems and cognitive function in *Yvain, ou le chevalier au lion* as a socially engaged text. We may begin recalling some provocative points made by Peter Haidu in his book *Lion-queue-coupée: l'écart symbolique chez Chrétien de Troyes* (Geneva: Droz, 1972), which bears specifically upon the semiotic status of the lion in this romance.

Haidu's *Lion-queue-coupée* has in common with his article "The Hermit's Pottage" this virtue: it calls attention less to specific symbols themselves than to the very symbol-making process in Chrétien's art. In the earlier work, Haidu is less concerned than in the later with the power of Chrétien's art to refer to, or to act upon, the real things (or their meanings) of the poet's social world. Along with previous readers of Yvain, Haidu recognizes the various symbolic investments in the lion, but especially calls attention to Chrétien's tendency to exploit the mobility and polyvalence of this symbol in a spirit of play that seems to elude even the burden of the sacred elements of his *matière*. Haidu equates this play with the "literary" function of the text

> En effet, le champ sémiologique de la religion y est traité comme une source parmi d'autres, également génératrices de sens, une source en compétition avec d'autres champs également accessibles et valables. Et, comme pour les autres valeurs symboliques, le sens produit par l'allégorie exégétique peut être refusé. Car Chrétien, après son renvoi à cette tradition iconographique et mystique, s'amuse de son lion et nous amuse avec son lion. L'animal, un moment entouré d'autres signes iconographiques (le serpent, son geste d'humilité, etc.) un moment rehaussé comme véhicule d'allégorie christologique, redevient, dans l'épisode suivant, non pas un simple et banal lion, il est vrai, mais un pur lion littéraire, féroce et tendre, symbole de fidélité et de férocité, de sentimentalité, d'ironie, et de farce, symbole de tout sauf du Christ ou de n'importe quelle valeur religieuse prise avec gravité. (p. 72)

> Indeed, the semantic field of religion is treated there merely as one source among others which also generate meanings; hence, it is a source competing with other fields that are equally accessible and valid. And, like the other symbolic values, the meaning produced by exegetical allegory can be denied. For, after evoking the iconographical and mystical tradition, Chrétien amuses both himself and his audience with his lion. At one moment accompanied by other iconographical signs (the serpent, his gesture of humility, and so forth), and at another moment exalted as the vehicle of a Christological allegory, this animal once again becomes, in the following episode, not a simple and banal lion, to be sure, but a purely literary lion—ferocious and tender, a symbol of fidelity and ferocity, of sentimentality and of irony and farce, a symbol of anything but Christ or any other religious value that must be taken seriously.

Like most readers of *Yvain*, I am grateful for Haidu's remarks about the semiotic status of Chrétien's lion, and I would add that this lion may be called a "metastable" sign, in the sense that Claude Gandelman has given to that term: a metastable sign is one whose status and nature fluctuate as we perceive it, and such fluctuation constitues its primary poetic function. Gandelman writes:

> Although metastable patterns do not constitute a system in the sense that language and sub-languages like traffic signs or pathological symptoms constitute systems of signs, ... metastable visual figures may

well have their equivalents or parallels in the realm of language proper. In fact . . . there seem to exist a category of words and perhaps even sentences which present a semantic reversibility and which, therefore, can be termed 'metastable'.[15]

Gandelman extends his notion of metastability to the very notion of conventional sign, composed of signifier and signified:

Metastable patterns, though they form an exceptional subgroup within the larger category of the verbal or visual sign, may exhibit a significant feature shared by all signs. Indeed, is not the internal relation which defines the sign $\frac{Signifié}{Signifiant}$ (if one adopts the Saussurian scheme) a metastable relation? Though linguists speak of the 'interaction' between *signifié* and *signifiant*, would not 'metastability' be a more proper term? (p. 83)

Perhaps we may follow Gandelman's lead and suggest that as a metastable sign, the lion is a condensation of several distinct referents, each belonging to a different discourse, and in that sense Chrétien's lion may be indeed be taken, as Haidu suggests, as an instance of the play of "literary" discourse that puts other discourses into play as well.

However, the notion of literature (whether serious or playful) is always problematical for readers of medieval texts, where no discursive concept is to be found which corresponds to the modern and essentially romantic meaning of that word. If the term "medieval literature" invites, by its very incongruousness, reflection of a somewhat more historical sort, Haidu's book indicates one direction that such reflection might take (though Haidu himself does not take it):

S'il y a une méditation sérieuse sur la nature humaine et sur les rapports de l'individu et des valeurs sociales qui le régissent—hypothèse que je ne prétends pas avoir traitée dans ce travail, mais que je crois profondément vraie pour Chrétien de Troyes—elle n'a rien du didactisme religieux si fréquent au moyen-âge. Elle ressemble bien plus au jeu gratuit qu'est toute littérature avant d'être contemplation métaphysique ou affirmation morale. (p. 72)

If there is here a serious meditation on human nature and on the relationship between the individual and the social values that govern him or her—this is a hypothesis that I do not claim to have treated in the present work, but one that I believe profoundly true for Chrétien de Troyes—this meditation has nothing of the religious didacticism that is so common in the Middle Ages. It resembles much more that gratuitous play that literature is before it is metaphysical contemplation or moral affirmation.

I have already tried to show how Chrétien inscribes into *Yvain*, along with the "heap" of didactic religious values associated with the lion, a more "tree-like" set of classifications based upon *differentiae* of natural laws which are not in themselves moral, though they are the very preconditions of moral action in the world. As for Haidu's claim for Yvain and for "all literature" as "gratuitous play," let us not dismiss it out of hand, but hold it in suspension in order to draw attention to certain cultural tendencies in late twelfth century France called "heraldry" or "blazon" which are intimately connected with vernacular poetry (and with the rise romance in particular) and which will perhaps furnish some hints as to the changing nature and cultural function of "literary" signs in Chrétien's context.

Let us begin by recalling an episode that holds something in common with the scene where the maidens recognize Yvain by his scar: in *Erec et Enide*, Gauvain and Guenevere debate about the consequences that may be drawn from the dents in Yder's shield. These dents may be considered as a kind of equivocal text, rather, as a kind of "indexical"[16] pre-text for a story that remains to be told (and written). Like hieroglyphs, petroglyphs, or caroglyphs, these dents predicate, though incompletely, certain events that have transpired: given that swords have dented metal, we may infer for certain that a combat has taken place, and we can even imagine what that combat must have been like. However, the truth itself of "what happened" is disclosed to these fictive readers not through induction, but through "what happens" in subsequent (fictive) history.

But not all shields in Chrétien's romances convey the same message, nor do they all signify by the same indexical mode. Other shields, for example, produce meaning because of designs or figures of animals *painted* upon them and no longer because of physical accidents altering their form. These painted designs and figures are no more determined, in their selection, by either the form or the function of the shield itself than is the writer's selection of words materially determined by parchment or paper. Sometimes a shield is painted with a kind of protonarrative emblem recalling a tale about its bearer, in which case it serves its reader as an *aide-mémoire*. Such is the case with Yder himself, when he reappears in Chrétien's *Chevalier de la charrette*. Here, Yder's shield is "blazoned" as follows by some knights who are watching a joust:

> "Et veez vos celui qui porte
> An son escu pointe une porte?
> Si sanble qu'il s'an isse uns cers.
> Par foi, ce est li rois Yders."
> (ll. 5799–5802)

"And do you see the one who carries a shield with a gate painted on it? A stag seems to be emerging from it. In faith, that is King Yder."

This shield not only identifies its bearer, whose identity is otherwise concealed by armor, but also begins to tell a story that is anaphorically related to that earlier episode in *Erec et Enide*, where, during the customary hunt for the White Stag, Yder affronts Guenevere and summons, thereby, his future defeat by Erec during a quest that finally leads to Erec's marriage with Enide. In other words, this shield has several semiotic functions: first, it conveys an image; second, it evokes a set of narrative circumstances that serve to identify its bearer; third, by recalling a story in which Yder was implicated, it serves as an intertextual sign anaphorically linking the present instance of narrative discourse with a corpus of other romances. In their aggregate, these functions constitute a code.

There is yet another kind of shield, which neither signifies materially (as does the dented shield of Yder interpreted by Gauvain and Guenevere) nor refers narratively or metaphorically to its bearer. Rather, such a shield identifies its bearer by a totally arbitrary, nonnarrative or nongenetic bond between image as *signifier* and bearer as *signified*, which is to say that their conventional designs or figures bave no metaphorical, nor any other apparent relationship to the individual that they serve to identify. This is a kind of semiosis that Peirce calls the "symbolic." Such is apparently the case, for example, when Erec recognizes Kay in the forest by his arms, though Kay does not recognize Erec, because his arms, lent to him by Enide's impoverished father, are not marked but plain. In this case, the disclosure of identity by one heraldic "text" and the impenetrable blankness of the other are important details to the characters themselves, since Erec actually *declines* to declare his identity to Kay by naming himself (ll. 3949–71). In the *Charrette*, we encounter a whole series of shields whose heraldic emblems, though perfectly arbitrary, still serve to identify their bearers, though only to those initiated into the art of "reading" such emblems, as is the case with these knights watching a tournament:

> Antr'ax dïent: "Veez vos or
> Celui a cele bande d'or
> Par mi cel escu de bernic?
> C'est Governauz de Roberdic.
> Et veez vos celui aprés,
> Qui an son escu pres a pres
> A mise une aigle et un dragon?
> C'est li fils le roi d'Arragon
> Qui venuz est an ceste terre
> Por pris et por enor conquerre."
> (ll. 5773–82)

They say to each other, "Do you see the one with the stripe of gold on a burnished shield? That is Governauz de Roberdic. And do you see the one following him, who has side by side on his shield an eagle and a dragon? That is the son of the King of Arragon, who has come to this land for esteem and to win honor."

That such heraldic designs and emblems have no intrinsic personal or symbolic relationship to their bearer is implicit in what Gerard J. Brault says of this shield in the *Charrette* : "The King of Aragon, whose son's arms are blazoned here, is a stock character in Arthurian romance and was doubtless associated with Spain only in the vaguest sort of way in Chrétien's mind. At any rate, the eagle preying on (?) the dragon in this shield has nothing whatsoever to do with the Royal Arms of Aragon (or, four pales gules) attested on the seal of Ramon Berengar IV of Aragon in 1157."[17]

If we may consider different kinds of emblems in Chrétien's texts as kinds of texts in their own right, each calling for a different hermeneutical response, let us step back somewhat and make some brief comparisons of these textual modes, not only within Chrétien, but starting with the *Roland* as well. Roland himself, as I have said elsewhere, is a hero fully identifiable to his peers by both his actions and his words, and his story exemplifies a basic transparency and eternal presence of truth in a heroic world where Christians are always right and pagans are wrong. Roland's myth is also a myth of iconic significations: he wields a sword given to him by God, and his conquests translate God's will into historical realities of time and space whose significations are sanctified, necessary, and self-evident. Charlemagne, by contrast, is caught in a world where both words and things have suddenly become equivocal, yet where signification still remains possible when a proper interpretive effort is made, as occurs when Charlemagne "reads" Roland's pre-grammatical petroglyphs at Ronceval and construes their meaning into a true heroic story. Charlemagne is the first, indeed, the primeval reader of the *chanson de geste*. However, since the meanings of words and things are equivocal and transient, Charlemagne also expresses a cultural need to determine and to *fix* the meaning of the catastrophe at Ronceval, and this need is exemplified in his gesture of removing the hearts from the bodies of Roland and the twelve peers in order to place them in a white marble tomb, which presumably will bear written inscriptions. The myth of Charlemagne in the *Roland* carries us from a culture where iconic signs are the privileged bearers of truth to a culture of written symbols, in the sense that Peirce gives to that term: that is, of signs which signify purely arbitrarily, and by no material necessity.[18] The myth of Charlemagne therefore carries us up to, but not fully into, a poetics of *grammatica*.

In Chrétien, we find emblems which signify both iconically and indexically, as in the *Roland*, but in addition we encounter heroes bearing emblems on their shields whose relationship to their personal identities is *purely* arbitrary, or symbolic, in Peirce's sense of the term. Inner identity and outer emblem are distinct from each other and are related in the same way that letters are arbitrarily related to vocal sounds, and that sounds as signifying words, in turn, are only arbitrarily related to the intellections they signify. Moreover, the relationship between armorial signifier and the identity that it signifies cannot be merely witnessed or remembered, it must be read by a reader initiated into the code of the noble armorial text. Chrétien's mythical world of knights and ladies now includes a hidden myth of *grammatica*. Such a system exploits *differences* in a special cognitive way. In *grammatica*, differences between letters arbitrarily correspond to differences between vocal sounds; these, in turn, become the arbitrary foundation for *semantic* differences, though all three orders are distinct and are in a relationship of hierarchy favoring the semantic. Without necessarily considering him as a "source," let us nevertheless see how Augustine ponders the "infancy" (*infans* means "nonspeaking" in Latin) of *grammatica* and its subsequent inauguration as the repository of past human culture:

> When reason had gone further, it noticed that of those oral sounds which we used in speaking and which it had already designated by letters, there were some which by a varied modulation of the parted lips flowed clear and pure from the throat without any friction; that others acquired a certain kind of sound form the diversified pressure of the lips; and that there were still other sounds, which could not issue forth unless they were conjoined with these. Accordingly, it denominated the letters in the order of their exposition: vowels, semivowels, and mutes. In the next place, it took account of syllables. Then words were grouped into eight classes and forms; and their entire evolvement, purity and articulation were skillfully and minutely differentiated . . . The science of grammar could now have been complete. But since by its very name it proclaims that it knows letters — indeed on this account it is called "literature" in Latin — it came to pass that whatever was committed to letters as worth remembering, necessarily pertained to it.[19]

The point I wish to make here is that Chrétien's romances lead us far beyond the semiotic realm of the *Roland*, where the presence of signifiers to their signifieds could mediate the presence of humans in the creation to their creator; Chrétien's romances lead us to a system of heraldic emblems whose power to signify the presence of human to human within the social group is a priori purely conventional and arbitrary. As we go from the bundle or "heap" of religious and moral interpretations of animality to the Porphyrean "tree" of *differentiae* by which we are invited to think logically about animals as signs, and finally to a system of *purely* arbitrary differences constituting the code of heraldic emblems, we move closer and closer to a social universe whose ontological landscape rests upon a properly textual or grammatical foundation. In such a realm, animality becomes implicated as signs in a "grammar" not of letters, but of emblems which serve to identify *differences* within a social order: first, differences between noble between families and clans, and, later, differences between other social groups within a hierarchy of classes. This is another way of suggesting, with John F. Benton, that "writing put the -ism in feudalism."[20] If humans are animals, they are social animals. And if they are social animals, their sociability is determined by writing. I have already stressed in chapter one how the archival movement of Philippe-Auguste inscribed knights, through their seals, into a textually defined set of social obligations. The development of seals and armorials in medieval culture was practically synonymous. As Michel Pastoureau puts it, "pour la période médiévale, il ne peut y avoir héraldique sans sigillographie"[21] ("for the medieval period, there could be no heraldry without a sigillography"). Indeed, though it is customary for historians to explain the rise of heraldry from the simple necessity of identifying combatants, it seems clear that the use of seals both preceded armorials and nourished their elaboration. A seal, moreover, did not need a shield to be displayed, and for that reason could even be assigned to women: "Les premières armoiries féminines apparaissent dès la seconde moitié du XIIe siècle" (p. 29) ("The first feminine armorials appeared already in the second half of the twelfth century"). Later came the other social groups:

"Le développement de l'usage du sceau a eu pour principale conséquence l'adoption d'armories non seulement par les femmes et les clercs, mais surtout par les roturiers. Les plus anciennes armoiries de bourgeois et gens des métiers voient le jour un peu avant le milieu du XIIIe siècle en France et dans les pays rhénans et flamands . . . Elles prolifèrent au siècle suivant, au point que sur l'ensemble des armoiries médiévales actuellement recensées, deux sur trois sont bourgeoises." (p. 30)

The development of the use of the seal had as its principal consequence the adoption of armorials not only by women and by the clergy, but especially by the non-nobles. The oldest armorials of bourgeois and tradesmen came to light shortly before the middle of the thirteenth century in France and in Flanders and the Rhineland. They proliferated in the following century, to the point where in the totality of these medieval armorials that we know of now, two out of three are bourgeois.

Clearly, heraldic emblems were divorced very early from their semiotic function within the chivalric combat or joust and functioned as emblems whose "differences" no longer articulated species and *genera* in the natural world, but rather designated *social* groups within the social world. These new signs expressed the economic status of their bearers as well, for, during the age of "classic" blazon in the thirteenth century, heraldic emblems were compiled into systematic codices called "rolls of arms," which served to define social groups and their possessions, rigorously classified according to conventional (as opposed to natural) *differentiae* between emblems. Constituted as a strictly conventional visual language, these rolls of arms expressed the totality of the social order in the form of a book. This book also contained another strictly conventional *verbal* language called "blazon." Blazon is the technical language employed to describe, for judicial purposes, heraldic emblems.

Paradoxically, the more social identity and political power became nominal—that is, based on a person's name—the more those who held or acquired power dialectically sought to invest their names with an authority which was not arbitrary, but based upon a myth of archaic origins expressed as agnatic lineage.[22] Hence, the rise of heraldry, in which a system of differences functioned completely *arbitrarily* that is, with no genetic or even narrative connection between the heraldic emblem and the individual it now designated, summoned forth genealogical texts which might restore to names an "etymological" power, in the medieval sense of that term. In other words, genealogies and rolls of arms may be understood as contrary semiotic systems within the same culture, the one summoned forth dialectically by the other.

I suggest that there was yet another contrapuntal semiotic movement, this one instigated by the clergy, whose purpose was somehow to master or "reclaim" the errant social and literary symbolism within twelfth-century culture by reinvesting its emblems with *religious* signification, and the tension between these two cultural motives in the Grail literature has recently been studied by Alexandre Leupin.[23] Twelfth-century society tended more and more to exploit the system of natural *differentia* rhetorically, and not just logically. Writing about the relationship between etymology (in the medieval sense) and heraldry, R. Howard Bloch says of the heraldic emblem that "here the logician's concept of physical property as that which distinguishes an object from all others in its class along with the rhetorician's notion of correct imposition are both pertinent to the particularized relation between the prince, his family, and its singular sign" (p. 77). Precisely because such signification is understood to be arbitrarily imposed on the heraldic emblem, heraldry is a textual system which is like that of *grammatica* itself, since grammarians too were very clear in their understanding that meanings are always "imposed" upon vocal sounds and, by extension, upon written letters signifying those sounds. However, the criteria for construing and manipulating such impositions were, as Chrétien understood, finally rhetorical, and not logical.

We perhaps recognize in the preceding discussion a problem that Claude Lévi-Strauss formulated in his theory of totemism. The relationship, according to Lévi-Strauss, between the true totemic animal or plant and the social group that it signifies is not one of common origin or shared identity of substance; nor is the totemic emblem a sacred manifestation of some divine presence because "le contacte direct . . . c'est-à-dire, la relation de contigüité, est contraire à l'esprit de l'institution: le totem ne devient tel qu'à condition d'être d'abord éloigné"[24] ("direct contact, that is to say, the relationship of contiguity, is contrary to the spirit of the institution. The totem does not become such unless it is distanced"). The totemic object is a priori an arbitrary sign, and Lévi-Strauss seems to follow Durkheim's suggestion that recourse by a society to plants and animals as totemic objects is only secondary to the system itself, which is entirely predetermined from within culture:

> Mais pourquoi le totémisme fait-il appel à des animaux ou à des plantes? Durkheim a donné de ce phénomène une explication contingente: la permanence et la continuité du clan requièrent seulement un emblème, qui peut être – et qui doit être à l'origine – un signe arbitraire, assez simple pour que n'importe quelle société puisse en concevoir l'idée, même à défaut de moyens d'expression artistique. Si l'on a ultérieurement "reconnu" dans ces signes la représentation d'animaux ou de plantes, c'est que les animaux et les plantes sont présents, accessibles, faciles à signifier. Pour Durkheim, par conséquent, la place que fait le totémisme aux animaux et aux végétaux constitue une sorte de phénomène à retardement. (p. 87)

> But why does totemism draw upon animals or plants? Durkheim gave a contingent explanation of this phenomenon: the permanence and the continuity of the clan require only an emblem, which may be – and which must originally be – an arbitrary sign that is simple enough so that any society may conceive the idea, even in the absence of means of artistic expression. If afterward some have "recognized" in these signs the representation of animals or plants, it is because the animals and plants are present, accessible, and easy to signify. For Durkheim, consequently, the place given to animals and plants in totemism is a delayed phenomenon.

In such a perspective, the totemic object may be said to function "grammatically," as words do, which is simply to resituate Lévi-Strauss's totemic theory in its original site of development, which was structural linguistics – this, despite Lévi-Strauss's claim that "le totémisme est une unité artificielle, qui existe seulement dans la pensée de l'éthnologue, et à quoi rien de spécifique ne correspond au dehors" (p. 14) ("totemism is an artificial entity, which exists only in the thought of the ethnologist, and something to which nothing specific outside corresponds"). Perhaps we may say that all totemic systems may be considered as a kind of *grammatica*, imagined as the *nursery* of culture, as John of Salisbury portrayed that institution. Perhaps too, common heraldic emblems such as lion, dragon, angel, crane, bull, dog, devil, wild man, stag, chicken, and dolphin are articulated on the shields of men and in rolls of arms in such a way that all symbolic, ontological, and ethical investments are banished, precisely so that their bearers may be integrated as empty but repeatable (and inheritable) grammatical signs into the roll of arms as a social text.

Moreover, it follows that in order to enter as a grammatical sign into a cultural text—or a textual culture—that is constituted by other heraldic signs, the heraldic sign must be capable of being inflected. Such indeed is the case. For instance, a heraldic lion can appear running (*courant*) or charging (*rampant*): he can wear a collar or a crown; he can have a single or forked tale (*lion a la coue fourchiée*); the lion may appear single or in multiples (e.g., *a siz lionceus*); such lions may be distributed in numerous distinct locations within the space of the shield. Presumably, if aristocrats really bore such emblems on their shields, it was because they now recognized (as Roland, Ganelon, and Pinabel did not) that the conduct of warfare must remain subject to laws expressed in and by the social text: the shield's *signifying* function within an armorial and archival system tended, therefore, to subsume its military function within the social order.

The idea that individuals become significant—even to themselves—by their expression within the group, and by extension that groups themselves become significant in their combinations with *other* groups, seems to be central to later twelfth-century literate culture, and such a semiotic notion is amplified and refined in the new emphasis, among theoreticians of language in the same period, upon syntax as a determinant of signification. Not only does a conventional word represent itself (as in the statement, " 'horse' ends in 'e' "), it also "stands for" a concept; but the concept becomes significant only when it is uttered in a sentence. To quote an anonymous twelfth-century commentator on Priscian, "If a word (*nomen*) is part of a sentence, therefore it is a part existing in a sentence. Therefore, if it is *not* a part existing in a sentence, it is not a word. Therefore, unless there is a sentence, there is not a word."[25] As Yvain himself illustrates by his own destiny, if a man regresses from his social status, he loses all *sens*, in every sense.

Thus, the heraldic emblem is a very peculiar kind of text. On the one hand, it identifies a knight not by his individual nature or by his feats, but within an a priori cultural "syntax;" that is to say, it is a text that embodies nothing of the intrinsic substance of its bearer. It is a social *outside* of an identity which has willingly concealed itself *inside* a coat of armor and has become, thereby, private and inscrutable. This ambivalent function of the heraldic text both to enclose and to disclose a human identity is expressed, moreover, by an interesting lexical ambivalence in certain terms in blazon vocabulary. According to Brault, the term *conoissance* in blazon means "arms or distinctive device on a heraldic shield" (p. 148). It also means "difference." *Conoistre* means "to recognize a coat of arms" or to "recognize a person by his coat of arms" ("*Qui por les armes nel conoissent*," *Cligès*, l. 3488) Yet these terms are synonymous, according to Brault, with the set *desconoissance* and *desconoistre*, which not only mean "arms or distinctive device on a heraldic shield," and difference," and "to differentiate," but also "disguise," or "to disgise one's arms" (p. 168). Here the notion of "difference" implies not *differentiae* constituting a natural system, but rather that more radical alterity of the heraldic text to the individual subject that by convention it is enlisted to signify. In other words, the discourse of natural science is being preempted by a new and very powerful kind of social discourse instituted to assert a new class structure within the social group.

That heraldry and blazon are systems of culture which were constituted during the second half of the twelfth century is a matter of common agreement among historians of the phenomenon. That is to say, seals, money (coins also bear heraldic seals), and romances all tend to instigate a new kind of "general" textuality by which the social order is signified and by which power is mediated. There is no doubt but that Chrétien's own *oeuvre* was one of the instigating powers behind this semiological revolution, though in such complex historical processes it is difficult to distinguish clearly between cause and effect.

Although much remains to be understood about the relationship between romance and heraldry, it is probably safe to say that they belong to, and express, a single "textual community," in the sense that Brian Stock gives to that term.[26] This textual community is the high aristocracy of twelfth-century France, and we may assume that the discursive practices peculiar to this aristocracy were perceived even by those who practised them as being a part of a larger mosaic. As Stock writes:

An important consequence of literacy in any human community arises from the area of social organization. Relationships between the individual and the family, the group, or the wider community are all influenced by the degree to which society acknowledges written principles of operation. Literacy also affects the way people conceptualize such relations, and these patterns of thought inevitably feed back into the network of real interdependencies. (p. 88)

We should not infer, however, that a given text merely defines or represents a given textual community within its context; indeed, the textual performance instigates change or reform *within* a community as well. As Stock says, "What was essential to a textual community was not a written version of a text, although that was sometimes present, but an individual, who having mastered it, then utilized it for reforming a group's thought and action" (p. 90). For this reason, twelfth-century culture was a mosaic of many textual communities, but a mosaic whose elements and forms were dynamic, rather than static. We may assume that Chrétien's patrons sponsored his writings in order to inculcate, perhaps above all by a new sense of play and by deliberate pleasure in the arbitrariness of verbal signs—even of privileged cultural signs such as "lion"—a new set of ideological values within the social group as a whole.

The sign "lion" functions in Chrétien's *Yvain* as a remarkable shifter between several discourses: that of an allegorical moral system, that of a natural or "physical" system, and that of a new and purely social system that we may call heraldic or totemic. Early heraldic emblems tend to exploit animals for their "differences" — Pastoureau estimates their frequency at sixty percent (p. 29) — and among these the lion and the eagle are supreme. As Rodney Dennys writes:

> An analysis of French seals and enamels between 1127 and 1300 shows the Lion as by far the most popular charge in heraldry after the ordinaries, with two hundred and twenty different examples of the Lion rampant and forty of the Lion passant (although many of these may have been meant to be Leopards). The earliest example is the blue shield with six little gold Lions rampant which Henry I gave to Geoffrey of Anjou in 1127, and there is reason to think that Henry himself used one or more lions as his emblem.[27]

The lion had already become, by Chrétien's time, the emblem of the emblematic, and Chrétien takes great pleasure in "shifting" the lion's discursive status before our very eyes. If, at first, the lion in the woods signifies Yvain's redeemed animal nature, as soon as Yvain disguises his identity during his quest in the social world for renewed honor and becomes an unnamed *chevalier au lion*, the lion becomes inescapably a heraldic emblem, even though he his not yet painted on Yvain's shield. However, Chrétien holds his audience on the boundary between cognitive systems as long as he can, refusing to let the lion become a passive bearer of significations. Each time he leaps into the fray, the lion is both a real causal force in the world and a perfectly conventional *lion rampant* of heraldic armorials. Elsewhere, a maiden seeks Yvain as her champion in a legal dispute with her sister although this maiden knows of the knight only by hearsay. She arrives at a castle where Yvain has just slept, she explains that she is looking for " 'the one whom I have never seen, I believe, nor known. But he has a lion with him, and I am told that I can place great trust in him' " (ll. 4902–6). Lunette directs her to yet another castle, where once once again she asks for "the one who will never be without his lion, as I have heard" (ll. 5020–21). The host advises the maiden her to follow their tracks through the woods. Is there not something comical about a maiden in distress tracking down a knight and his heraldic lion in the woods? Perhaps the best semiotic trick that Chrétien plays occurs when *le chevalier au lion* arrives at a castle bearing a shield which does not have the *image* of a lion painted on it, but bearing, rather, the *real* lion, which has been wounded in combat. The lord of the castle and his men have no trouble recognizing this *chevalier au lion!* In Yvain's afterlife in later romances he will bear a shield on which the lion has assumed his proper status as a conventional heraldic emblem, though one which also hearkens back to this founding relationship. As Brault writes:

> In Chrétien de Troyes, Yvain is, of course, known as *Le Chevalier au Lion* in the romance of the same name. Nowhere in the latter work, however, does the hero bear a shield decorated with a lion device.

Nevertheless, the fact that Yvain rescued a lion from a fiery serpent and that the grateful animal became the hero's companion and protector in this story resulted in traditional arms featuring a lion. In *Durmart le Galois*, for example, Yvain and all his retinue bear arms alluding to this event. (p. 49)

I would suggest, then, that the sense of play that Haidu equates with Chrétien's *littérarité* is a reflection of his careful experimentation with the semiotics of aristocratic power in twelfth-century northern France. Chrétien writes for a new textual community seeking after new kinds of poetic (and social) signs. The semiotic metastability of Yvain's lion expresses a cultivated dynamism which characterizes Chrétien's manipulation of inherited sources throughout his career. That the lion should *now* express scriptural or classical symbolic meanings, *now* signify lioninity as a species among other species, and *now* serve as a heraldic emblem—by such mutations in the lion's semiotic status, we may see that Chrétien has taken a sign privileged by those in power in his culture in order underscore the arbitrary and social basis of all conventional paradigms of human understanding. Chrétien's playful endorsement of relativism in socially determined signs and his artistic pleasure in such arbitrariness were surely welcome in a culture whose leaders were actively seeking ways to limit the ravages of chivalric warfare and to bring together merchants from "different" lands in commercial *foires* where all value was relative and where bargaining, arbitration, and exchange, within this relativity, could bring profit to all.

To conclude, we may find in Yvain's relationship to his lion rich cultural resonances which define, I would propose, Chrétien's own relationship to literature—not "literature" in the modern sense of that term, but to *litteratura* as *grammatica* and as culture. Thus, the more progress Yvain makes toward his redemption as a member of the social order and as a spouse in the marriage that he had transgressed, the more the lion's utility as an emblem expressing Yvain's noble animal nature is supplanted by the lion as a purely conventional heraldic emblem. Indeed, Chrétien quite simply drops the lion as a protagonist in the romance when Yvain becomes the social animal that he once was as a courteous, loving knight. Henceforth, the lion survives in the human world only as an enduring emblem of that yet more splendid animal: Yvain as a fighting, loving, loyal, and married man.

The closure of *Yvain, ou le chevalier au lion* is the fulfillment of a social contract that includes many ethical dimensions: that of an economy of just values and prices, that of a restricted aristocracy living up to its new mandate to be fruitful and multiply, and that of an individual to his own identity as that identity must be mediated by and perfected in the social group. Given that the conclusion of this story points to fulfillment of heroic identity within the social group and not to fulfillment in transcendence, Chrétien's *Yvain* is also the fulfillment of vernacular poetic language now serving as as the living vehicle of a perfected social consciousness. This fictive victory of a knight over flaws in his own animal nature is a true victory over the confusion, among inherited sources, of a poetic vision whose ends are at once ideal *and* immanent to the social order. In this sense Chrétien's *Yvain* may be considered as the very centerpiece of twelfth-century French humanism.

Notes

Notes

Introduction

1. Paul Zumthor, *Langue et techniques poétiques à l époque romane* (Paris: Klincksieck, 1963).

2. See Eugene Vance, "Roland, Charlemagne, and the Poetics of Memory," in *Textual Strategies*, ed. Josue Harrari (Ithaca: Cornell Univ. Press, 1978), pp. 374–403.

3. Robert-Henri Bautier, "Le règne de Philippe Auguste dans l'histoire de France," in *La France de Philippe Auguste: Le temps des mutations*, ed. Robert-Henri Bautier (Paris: Editions du C. N. R. S., 1982), p. 17. See also Eugene Vance, "Medievalisms and Models of Textuality," *Diacritics* 13, (1985), pp. 55–64.

4. For a recent study of the book in medieval culture, not only as a material object but also as a determinant of thought and of semiosis, see Jesse M. Gellrich, *The Idea of the Book in the Middle Ages: Language Theory, Mythology, and Fiction* (Ithaca: Cornell Univ. Press, 1985).

5. Hans W. Frei, *The Eclipse of Biblical Narrative: A Study in Eighteenth and Nineteenth Century Hermeneutics* (New Haven: Yale Univ. Press, 1972), pp. 243–44.

6. Wilhelm Dilthey, "The Rise of Hermeneutics," trans. Fredric Jameson, *New Literary History* 3 (1972), p. 233.

7. Augustine, *De doctrina christiana* (2.1.1,) trans. D. W. Robertson, Jr. (Indianapolis and New York: Bobbs-Merrill, 1958), p. 34.

8. Tzvetan Todorov, *La grammaire du Décaméron* (The Hauge: Mouton, 1969); Todorov, "La quête du récit," *Critique* 262 (1969), pp. 195–214; Julia Kristeva, *Le texte du roman* (The Hague: Mouton, 1970); Roland Barthes, "L'ancienne rhétorique," *Communications* 16 (1970), pp. 172–229; Eugene Vance, "The Modernity of the Middle Ages in the Future: Remarks on a Recent Book," *Romanic Review* 64 (1973), pp. 140–51.

9. Bernard Cerquiglini, "Eloge de la variante," *Langages* 69 (1983), pp. 25–35. I summarize this article closely in the lines that follow.

10. Emile Benveniste, *Problèmes de linguistique générale* (Paris: Gallimard, 1966), pp. 225–85; Bernard Cerquiglini, *La parole médiévale* (Paris: Minuit, 1981); Marie-Louise Ollier, "Le présent

du récit: temporalité et roman en vers," *Langue française* 40 (1978), pp. 99–112; C. Marchello-Nizia, "Ponctuation et 'unité de lecture' dans les manuscrits médiévaux, ou: je ponctue, tu lis, il théorise," *Langue française* 40 (1978), pp. 32–44.

11. Peter Haidu, "Text and History: The Semiosis of Twelfth-Century Lyric as Sociohistorical Phenomenon (Chrétien de Troyes: 'D'Amor m'a tolu')," *Semiotica* 33 (1981), pp. 1–62; see also Haidu, "The Hermit's Pottage: Deconstruction and History in *Yvain*," in *The Sower and His Seed: Essays on Chrétien de Troyes*, ed. Rupert J. Pickens (Lexington: French Forum, Publishers, 1983), pp. 127–45; E. Jane Burns, *Arthurian Fiction: Reading the Grail Cycle* (Columbus: Ohio State Univ. Press, 1985).

12. Hans Robert Jauss, *Literaturgeschichte als Provokation* (Frankfurt: Suhrkamp, 1973); Jauss, *Alterität und Modernität der mittelalterlichen Literatur* (Munich: Fink Verlag, 1977), pp. 11–66.

13. Erich Köhler, "De Rolle des niederen Rittertums bei der Entstehung der Trobadorlyrik," in *Esprit und arkadische Freiheit. Aufsätze aus de Welt der Romania* (Frankfurt and Bonn: Athenëum, 1966), pp. 9–27.

14. Denis de Rougemont, *Love in the Western World*, trans. Mongomery Belgion, revised and augmented edition (Princeton: Princeton Univ. Press, 1983); see also de Rougement, *Love Declared: Essays on the Myth of Love*, trans Richard Howard (Boston: Beacon Press, 1964).

15. Jacques Lacan, *Ecrits* (Paris: Le Seuil, 1966). Among Sigmund Freud's writings, an especially provocative text for medievalists is his *Jokes and their Relation to the Unconscious*, trans. James Strachey (New York: Norton, 1963). See, for example, R. Howard Bloch, "The Fabliaux, Fetishism and Freud's Jewish Jokes," *Representations* 4 (1983), pp. 1–26; and Eugene Vance, "Greimas, Freud and the Story of *Trouvère* Lyric," in *Lyric Poetry: Beyond the New Criticism* (Ithaca: Cornell Univ. Press, 1985), pp. 92–105.

16. Giorgio Agamben, *Stanze. La parola e il fantasma nella cultura occidentale* (Turino: Einaudi, 1977); Roger Dragonetti, *Le gai savoir dans la rhétorique courtoise* (Paris: Le Seuil, 1982). See also Jean-Charles Huchet, "Nom de la femme et écriture féminine au moyen-âge," *Poétique* 48 (1981), pp. 407–30; Huchet, "Les femmes troubadours ou la voix critique," *Littérature* 51 (1983), pp. 59–90.

17. See Charles Mela, " 'La lettre tue': cryptographie du Graal," *Cahiers de civilisation médiévale* 26 (1983), 209–22.

18. Alexandre Leupin, "Ecriture naturelle et écriture hermaphrodite: le 'De planctu naturae', un art poétique du XIIe siècle," *Digraphe* 9 (1976), pp. 118–41; Leupin, "Qui parle? Narrateurs et scripteurs dans la 'vulgate arthurienne,' " *Digraphe* 20 (1979), 89–109; Leupin, "La faille et l'écriture dans les 'Continuations du Perceval,' " *Le Moyen-Age* 92 (1982), pp. 237–69; Leupin, "Le ressassement: sur le 'Jeu de la Feuillée' d'Adam de la Halle," *Le Moyen-Age* 93 (1983), pp. 240–70.

Chapter 1. From *Grammatica* to a Poetics of the Text

1. Jean Frappier, *Chrétien de Troyes: L'homme et l'oeuvre* (Paris: Hatier, 1957), p. 8. For a discussion of the impact of writing on vernacular poetics, see Zumthor, *Lanque et techniques poétiques à l'époque romane*, pp. 27–69; Zumthor, *Essai de poétique médiévale* (Paris: Le Seuil, 1972), pp. 64–106; Zumthor, *Lanque, texte, énigme* (Paris: Le Seuil, 1975), pp. 25–88. For a recent study of Chrétien with regard to the prestige of classical literature, see Michelle Freeman, *The Poetics of* Translatio Studii *and* Conjointure: Chrétien de Troyes' "Cligès" (Lexington, Ky.: French Forum, Publishers, 1979). See also Michel Foucault, "What is an Author?" in *Textual Strategies: Perspectives in Post-Structural Criticism*, ed. Josué Harari (Ithaca: Cornell Univ. Press, 1979), pp. 141–60.

2. John of Salisbury, *Metalogicon* 1.13, ed. Clement C. J. Webb (Oxford: Clarendon Press, 1929); trans. G. McGarry (Berkeley and Los Angeles: Univ. of California Press, 1955) pp. 37–38.

3. William of Conches, *Glossae super Macrobius*, trans. Peter Dronke, in Fabula: *Explorations*

into the Uses of Myth in Medieval Platonism, Mittellateinsche Studien und Texte, vol. 9 (Leiden and Cologne: E. J. Brill, 1974), pp. 17, 68.

4. John of Salisbury, *Policraticus*, ed. Clement C. J. Webb (Oxford: Clarendon Press, 1929); trans. Joseph B. Pike, under the title *Frivolities of Courtiers and Footprints of Philosophers* (Minneapolis: Univ. of Minnesota Press, 1938), p. 6.

5. *Le roman de Thèbes*, ed. Guy Raynaud de Lage (Paris: Champion, 1969), vol. 1, ll. 9213-18.

6. Hugonis de Sancto Victore, *Didascalicon: De studio legendi: A Critical Text* 2.8, ed. Charles Henry Buttimer (Washington, D.C.: Catholic Univ. Press, 1939); trans. Jerome Taylor, under the title *The Didascalicon of Hugh of St. Victor* (New York and London: Columbia Univ. Press, 1961), pp. 91-92. See also Pierre Riché, *Ecoles et enseignement dans le Haut moyen-âge* (Paris: Aubier, 1979), pp. 247-48.

7. Douglas Kelly, "La spécialité dans l'invention des topiques," in *Archéologie du signe*, ed. Lucie Brind' Amour and Eugene Vance (Toronto: Pontifical Institute of Medieval Studies, 1982), pp. 102-3.

8. According to Frederick Goldin, "Le temps de la chronique dans la *Chanson de Roland*," VIII Congreso de la Société Rencesvals (Navarra: Institucion Principe de Viana, 1981), pp. 173-83, the use of the preterit in the *Roland* does correspond to an assertion of truth and authority bound up with written sources. However, Goldin shows that the dramatic exploitation of the preterit does not produce a rigorous diachronism. Rather, the preterit is employed in function of the dynamism of what Goldin calls the *situation de performance* of the audience listening to a poet. For this reason, the preterit alternates with other tenses in accordance with the dramatic movement of the *laisse* itself, and the preterit marks not only a past truth, but a future necessity as well. The preterit also functions in opposition to the present in such a way as to distinguish between external and internal or emotional states. Though Goldin does not say so, the preterit functions more like a mode (or a modal) than like a temporal marker. See also Minnette Grunmann-Gaudet, "The Representation of Time in the *Chanson de Roland*," in *The Nature of Medieval Narrative*, ed. Minnette Grunmann-Gaudet and Robin F. Jones (Lexington, Ky: French Forum, Publishers, 1980), pp. 77-98; and Eugene Vance, *Reading the* Song of Roland (Englewood Cliffs: Prentice-Hall, 1970), pp. 17, 71.

9. Cf. Emile Benveniste, "Les relations de temps dans le verbe français," in *Problèmes de linguistique générale*, vol. 1 (Paris: Gallimard, 1966), pp. 237-50.

10. It was a commonplace of medieval rhetorical theory to consider writing as a supplement to the voice. For example, St. Augustine writes that "since men could not be most firmly associated unless they conversed and thus poured, so to speak, their minds and thoughts back and forth to one another—saw that names, or meaningful sounds, had to be assigned to things, so that men might use the sense almost as an interpreter to link them together, in as much as they could not perceive one another's minds. But they could not hear the words of those not present. Therefore, reason, having carefully noted and discriminated all the sounds of the mouth and tongue, invented letters." *De ordine* 2.12.36, trans. Robert P. Russell, O.S.A., under the title *Divine Providence and the Problem of Evil* (New York: Cosmopolitan Science and Art Service, 1942), pp. 139-41. See also Thomas Aquinas, *Aristotle: On Interpretation. Commentary by St. Thomas and Cajetan*, trans. Jean T. Oesterle (Milwaukee: Marquette Univ. Press, 1962), 1.2.2, p. 24. Thomas writes, "If man had only sensitive cognition, which is of the here and now, such significant vocal sounds as the other animals use would be sufficient for him to live with others. But man also has the advantage of intellectual cognition, which abstracts from the here and now, and as a consequence, is concerned with things distant in place and future in time as well as things present according to time and place. Hence the use of writing was necessary so that he might manifest his conceptions to those who are distant according to place and to those who will come in future time."

11. In classical and medieval hermeneutics, the present tense is understood as privileged over other tenses in the disclosure of truth. Aristotle, for example, in his *Peri hermeneias* says that the

past and future tenses are not even verbs, but "cases" of verb. The verb in the present tense is the strongest assertion of immutable truth. See also Abelard, *Glossae super Peri ermenias*, ed. Bernhard Geyer, in *Beiträge zur Geschichte der Philosophie des Mittelalters* (Münster: Verlag der Aschendorffschen Verlagbuchhandlung, 1927), vol. 21, pt 3, p. 345. In other words, there are two "presents" in Chrétien's narrative discourse: the "present" of the voice of the temporal past and the atemporal "present" of truth being disclosed by the interpreting voice of the narrator.

12. Chrétien de Troyes, *Yvain, ou le chevalier au lion*, ed. Wendelin Foerster (Halle: Max Niemeyer, 1906), ll. 29–30. All translations in this study, unless otherwise indicated, are my own.

13. Marie-Louise Ollier, "Le présent du récit: temporalité et roman en vers," *Langue française* 40 (1978), p. 105.

14. Rupert T. Pickens, "Historical Consciousness in Old French Narrative," *French Forum* 4 (1979), p. 177.

15. Douglas Kelly, "*Matière* and *genera dicendi* in Medieval Romance," *Yale French Studies* 51 (1974), pp. 147–48.

16. Eugene Vance, "Roland, Charlemagne, and the Poetics of Memory," in *Textual Strategies: Essays in Post-Structural Criticism*, ed. Josué Harari (Ithaca: Cornell Univ. Press, 1979), pp. 401–3.

17. Chrétien de Troyes, *Le chevalier de la charrette*, ed. Mario Roques (Paris: Champion, 1958), ll. 1884–91.

18. Matilda T. Bruckner, in a forthcoming essay on the *Charrette* in *The Romances of Chrétien de Troyes*, ed. Douglas Kelly (Lexington, Ky.: French Forum, Publishers), sees Lancelot's refusal to disclose his name as a dramatization of Chrétien's own "strategy of concealment" in his narrative. See also Eugene Vance, "Love's Concordance: The Poetics of Desire and the Joy of the Text," *Diacritics* 5 (1975), especially pp. 40–41.

19. Rupert T. Pickens, *The Welsh Knight: Paradoxicality in Chrétien's Conte del Graal* (Lexington, Ky.: French Forum, Publishers, 1977), p. 138.

20. Quintilian, *Institutio oratoria* 10.3.26, ed. and trans. H. E. Butler (Cambridge: Harvard Univ. Press; London: Heinemann, 1936). Quintilian was eloquent about the struggles of writing well. The writer, he tells us, must labor in complete solitude, must bang his desk, bite his nails, and thrash his way through his text, reading and rewriting it many times over before presenting it before the public.

21. Eugene Vance, "Freud, Greimas and the Story of *Trouvère* lyric: Gace Brulé," in *Lyric Poetry: Beyond the New Criticism*, ed. Patricia Parker and Chaviva Hosek (Ithaca: Cornell Univ. Press, 1985), pp. 93–105.

22. Chrétien de Troyes, *Erec et Enide*, ed. Mario Roques (Paris: Champion, 1955), ll. 23–26.

23. Abelard, *Glossae secundum Petrum Abaelardum super Porphyrium*, ed. Bernhard Geyer, *Beiträge zur Geschichte der Philosophie des Mittelalters* (Münster: Verlag der Aschendorffschen Verlagsbuchhandlung, 1919), vol. 21, pt. 1, p. 20.

Chapter 2. *De voir dire mot le conjure*: Dialectics and Fictive Truth

1. Chrétien de Troyes, *Le roman de Perceval ou ce conte du graal*, ed. William Roach (Geneva and Paris: Droz, 1959), ll. 6409–14.

2. Many critics have detected a "dialectical" tendency in Chrétien's narrative art, but few have tried to deal with the relationship between logic or dialectics in romance in a substantial way. The most serious attempt to date that I know of is the article by Tony Hunt, "Aristotle, Dialectic, and Courtly Literature," *Viator* 10 (1979), pp. 95–129. See also Hunt's "The Dialectic of *Yvain*," *Modern Language Review* 72 (1977), pp. 285–99. The more recent article is useful for its summary of the development of logic in the twelfth century. Despite its rehearsal of the external data concerning

logic in the period, this article deals with the relationship between logic and poetics only super-ficially. For Hunt, the influence of dialectics is noticeable above all as the construing of dialogue in the form of argument—"the trend away from the form as a rhetorical method of presenting the truth to that of a dialectical method for stimulating inquiry into the truth," (p. 106)—and as the ex-ploitation of paradox and oppositions. Yet few of the examples that Hunt mentions in his article are specifically dialectical, as opposed to being merely rhetorical.

3. Peter Abelard, "Glosses on the *Peri hermeneias*," trans. Hans Arens, in *Aristotle's Theory of Language and its Tradition: Texts from 500 to 1750* (Amsterdam and Philadelphia: Benjamins, 1984), pp. 239–40.

4. J. Isaac, *Le Peri hermeneias en occident de Boèce à Saint Thomas: Histoire littéraire d'un traité d'Aristote* (Paris: Vrin, 1953), p. 65.

5. R. W. Hunt, *The History of Grammar in the Middle Ages*, ed. G. L. Bursill-Hall (Amster-dam: Benjamins, 1980), p. 21.

6. G. L. Bursill-Hall, *Speculative Grammars of the Middle Ages: The Doctrine of the* partes orationis *of the Modistae* (The Hauge and Paris: Mouton, 1971), p. 29.

7. For an account of the relationship between *grammatica* and poetics in the Middle Ages, see Paul Salmon, "Über den Beitrag des grammatischen Unterrichts zur Poetik des Mittelalters," *Archiv für das Studium der neueren Sprachen und Literaturen* 199 (1963), pp. 65–84.

8. Abelard, *Logica ingredientibus*, in *Philosophische Schriften*, ed. B. Geyer, *Beiträge zur Geschichte der Philosophie des Mittelalters* 21 (1919), p. 2.

9. The following discussion of Abelard and logic is indebted to the magnificent study by Jean Jolivet, *Arts du langage et théologie chez Abélard* (Paris: Vrin, 1969), pp. 29–62.

10. Gabriel Nuchelmans, *Theories of the Proposition: Ancient and Medieval Conceptions of the Bearers of Truth and Falsity* (Amsterdam and London: North Holland, 1973), pp. 26–27.

11. Given the nineteenth-century tendency to equate "modern" or romantic literature (that is, me-dieval and renaissance literature) with the discovery of the subjective nature of humans, there is a danger that critics of our own century will continue to conflate medieval theories of the individual and of understanding with romantic notions of subjectivity and selfhood. Two recent books ex-emplify this tendency. The first is by Colin Morris, *The Discovery of the Individual, 1050–1200* (London: SPCK, 1972). Like the romantics, who attributed simplicity and externality to premedieval theories of human understanding, Morris sees twelfth-century individualism as a Christian rejection of a "simpler" past in favor of a "more complex" structure of self-consciousness: "The simpler rules of the immediate past were no longer adequate, and the more distant culture of the ancients provided inspiration indeed, but not solutions which could be readily applied to the new society of Christen-dom. The situation produced, as such situations have done in other ages, a new self-consciousness, a capacity for individual evaluation and criticism, and in general a demand for individual initiative" (p. 160).

The other book is by Robert W. Hanning, *The Individual in Twelfth Century Romance* (New Ha-ven: Yale Univ. Press, 1977). Hanning proposes that there is a dialectical relationship between the exterior, social role of the knight as an "unreflective" warrior and the "interior" sentiment of love which is moral and discriminating. This dialectic "unfolds through three clearly defined phases, functioning somewhat like thesis, antithesis, and synthesis" (p. 62), and as "the outer world of prow-ess affects and is affected by the inner world of love and awareness" (p. 62), the synthesis that occurs takes the form of an individual who is socially responsible. Hanning supposes that a dialectical *Selbstbewusstsein* (Hanning does not use the term himself, but the concept is clearly there) is also the telos of the knight as hero of the poetic imagination: "The romance plot lacks any context larger than the lives of its protagonists; it permits the simultaneous presentation of external, heroic adven-tures and of an inner world in which the self-awareness born of love permits the control of martial impulses. . . . The imagined world of chivalric romance probes the condition and needs of its protagonists and their quest for full individuality with conviction and irony, hope and cynicism, earnestness and comedy" (p. 60).

12. Daniel Poirion, *Le merveilleux dans la littérature française du moyen-âge* (Paris: Presses Universitaires de France, 1982).

13. Matilda T. Bruckner, "The *Folie Tristan d'Oxford*: Speaking Voice, Written Text," *Tristania* 7 (1981-1982), pp. 47-59; see also Bruckner, "Truth in Disguise: The Voice of Renarration in the *Folie Tristan d'Oxford*," forthcoming.

14. In her recent book, *The Merveilleux in Chrétien de Troyes' Romances* (Geneva: Droz, 1976), Lucienne Carasso-Bulow says that Chrétien's *merveilleux* is an effect of juxtaposing contraries of "realistic and fantastic elements" (p. 137). I would not disagree with such claims, but suggest that what the author means by "realism" is a world constructed according to logical principles that became second nature to poets after Chrétien—and to their readers.

15. John of Garland, *The Parisiana Poetria*, ed. and trans. Traugott Lawler (New Haven and London: Yale Univ. Press, 1974), p. 101.

16. Douglas Kelly, "The Scope and Treatment of Composition in the Twelfth and Thirteenth Century Arts of Poetry," *Speculum* 41 (1966), p. 261. See also Kelly, *Sens and Conjointure in the Chevalier de la Charrette* (The Hauge and Paris: Mouton, 1966), pp. 88-94; and Kelly, "Theory of Composition in Medieval Narrative Poetry and Geoffrey of Vinsauf's *Poetria Nova*," *Medieval Studies* 31 (1969), pp. 117-48.

17. Peter Haidu, *Aesthetic Distance in Chrétien de Troyes: Irony and Comedy in Cligès and Perceval* (Geneva: Droz, 1968).

18. See Aristotle, on "Substance." in *The Categories*, trans. Harold P. Cook, Loeb Classical Library (1973), pp. 19-35. Boethius writes, "It can happen that something is brought into contention by comparison, as when there is doubt whether courage is better than justice. But this question must be put among questions involving accidents, because nothing but accident comes into play in comparisons, for only accident admits of more and less" (Boethius, *De topicis differentiis* 1.1178c, p. 36. See also Jolivet, pp. 109-11.

19. Chrétien's argument "from the whole" is a dialectical topic. See Boethius, *De topicis differentiis*, 2.1188a, p. 51.

Chapter 3. Selfhood and Substance in *Erec et Enide*

1. Eugene Vance, *Reading the* Song of Roland (Englewood Cliffs: Prentice Hall, 1970), pp. 11, 65.

2. Eugene Vance, "Chrétien's *Yvain* and the Ideology of Change and Exchange," in *Mervelous Signals: Poetics and Sign Theory in the Middle Ages* (Lincoln: Univ. of Nebraska Press, 1986).

3. Abelard, *Glossae super Porphyrium*, ed. Geyer, in *Beiträge zur Geschichte der Philosophie des Mittelalters*, vol. 21, pt. 1, p. 13.

4. Aristotle, *Categories*, p. 33. See Jolivet, p. 110, concerning the Latin expression of "change within itself:" *secundum sui mutationem*.

5. Kent Kraft, "Modernism in the Twelfth Century," *Comparative Literature Studies* 3 (1981), p. 289; Brian Stock, *The Implications of Literacy: Written Language and Models of Interpretation in the Eleventh and Twelfth Centuries* (Princeton: Princeton Univ. Press, 1983), pp. 517-21.

6. Georges Lavis, *L'expression de l'affectivité dans la poésie lyrique française du moyen âge (XIIe-XIIIe s.)* (Paris: Les Belles Lettres, 1972).

7. For a discussion of the relationship between the rhetoric of romance, the passions of the soul, and the social activities of love and war, see Eugene Vance, "Le combat érotique chez Chrétien de Troyes: de la figure à la forme," *Poétique* 12 (1972), pp. 544-71; See also Vance, "Signs of the City: Medieval Poetry as Detour," *New Literary History* 4 (1973), pp. 163-77.

8. Donald Maddox, *Structure and Sacring: The Systematic Kingdom in Chrétien's* Erec et Enide (Lexington, Ky.: French Forum, Publishers, 1978), pp. 116-19, 155-63.

9. Winthrop Wetherbee, *Platonism and Poetry in the Twelfth Century: The Literary Influence of the School of Chartres* (Princeton: Princeton Univ. Press, 1972), p. 190.

10. Karl-Heinz Bender, "L'essor des motifs du plus beau chevalier et de la plus belle dame dans le premier roman courtois," in *Lebenbendige Romania: Festschrift für Hans-Wilhelm Klein* (n.p., 1977), pp. 35-46.

11. Although any story coheres by logic of one kind or another, the *Roland* illustrates the breakdown of one logic and the inability of the poet, his characters, and his language, to pass to another. Recently, several critics have invoked the Greimassian "semiotic square" to illustrate the logical crisis in the *Chanson de Roland*: Pierre van Nuffel, "Problèmes de sémiotique interprétative: l'épopée," *Lettres Romanes* 27 (1973), pp. 150-62; Larry S. Crist, "Deep Structures in the Chansons de Geste," *Olifant* 3 (1975), pp. 3-35; Alison Goddard Elliott, "The Power of Discourse: Martyr's Passion and Old French Epic," *Medievalia et Humanistica* 11 (1982), pp. 39-60. Such descriptive methods are valid, but the historical dimension of this intellectual crisis is also important. As all of these critics know, the Greimassian semiotic square is a recasting of the Apuleian square of Aristotelian logic, specifically, of *On Interpretation*, ch. 10. See Alain de Libéra, "La sémiotique d'Aristote," in *Structures élémentaires de la signification*, ed. Frédéric Nef (Brussels: Editions Complexe, 1976), pp. 28-48. Given that Aristotelian logic, and most specifically, the *On Interpretation* had by now made important inroads into all aspects of intellectual life of the twelfth century, one difference between Chrétien and the *Roland* poet (and between the knights of romance and the barons of epic) is that the later heroes can and must, themselves, reason (intuitively, of course) according to patterns subtended by the Aristotelian logical square.

12. For an account of the important shifts in the conception of marriage that occurred in the twelfth century, see *Dictionnaire de théologie catholique*, s.v. "Mariage;" John T. Noonan, Jr., "The Power to Choose," *Viator* 4 (1973), pp. 419-34; Marie-Odile Métral, *Le mariage. Les hésitations de l'Occident* (Paris: Aubier, 1977); Georges Duby, *Le chevalier, la femme et le prêtre. Le mariage dans la France féodale* (Paris: Hachette, 1981).

13. Wetherbee, *Platonism and Poetry in the Twelfth Century*, p. 238-39. Wetherbee's remarks about Erec merit further quotation: "With the introduction of the quadrivium, all worldly activity is set in a new perspective, and he becomes a philosopher-king, for whom earthly dominion is only a stage in the realization of a higher objective . . . . The stress on transcendence is confirmed . . . by the description of Erec's scepter, made of a single emerald and carved with the images of all creatures . . . . The scepter represents an Edenic vision in which things are seen in their true natures and as a unity, as they were once beheld before the fall" (p. 239).

14. Reto Bezzola, *Le sens de l'amour et de l'aventure (Chrétien de Troyes)* (Paris: La jeune parque, 1947), p. 246.

Chapter 4. *Topos* and Tale

1. The following writings on topical theory have been useful to the present study: Otto Bird, "The Formalizing of the Topics in Medieval Logic," *Notre Dame Journal of Formal Logic* 1 (1960), pp. 138-49; Otto Bird, "The Tradition of the Logical Topics: Aristotle to Ockham," *Journal of the History of Ideas* 23 (1967), pp. 307-23. Certain of Bird's conclusions have been corrected by N. J. Pedersen, "Walter Burley, *De consequentiis* and the Origin of the Theory of Consequence," in *English Logic and Semantics From the End of the Twelfth Century to the Time of Ockham and Burleigh*, Acts of the 4th European Symposium on Medieval Logic and Semantics, Leiden-Nijmegen. 23-27 April 1979, ed. H. A. G. Braakhuis, C. H. Kneepkens, and I. M. de Rijk, in *Aristarium*, Supplementa 1 (Nijmegen: Ingenium Publishers), pp. 279-304. See Peter Jehn, ed., *Toposforschung: eine Dokumentation* (Frankfurt: Athenaum, 1972); Max L. Baeumer,

Toposforschung, Wege der Forschung, 395 (Darmstadt: Wissenschaftliche Buchgesellschaft, 1973). See also Eleonore Stump, *Boethius's De topicis differentiis. Translated, with Notes and Essays on the Text* (Ithaca: Cornell Univ. Press, 1978); Stump, "Dialectic in the Eleventh and Twelfth Centuries: Garlandus Compotista," *History and Philosophy of Logic* 1 (1980), pp. 1–18; Stump, "Topics: Their Development and Absorption into Consequences," in *The Cambridge History of Later Medieval Philosophy*, ed. Norman Kretzmann, Anthony Kenny, and Jan Pinborg (Cambridge: Cambridge Univ. Press, 1982); Stump, "Topics, Consequences, and Obligations in Ockham's *Summa logicae*," forthcoming; Stump "Abelard on the Topics," forthcoming; and Stump, "Logic in the Early Twelfth Century," forthcoming. Stump's writings are the most systematic attempts to deal with both the theory and place of topics in the history of logic. Her book contains a valuable bibliography on the subject. For an interesting study of the relationship between logical and rhetorical topics, see Michael C. Leff, "Boethius's *De differentiis topicis*, Book 4," in *Medieval Eloquence: Studies in the Theory and Practice of Medieval Rhetoric*, ed. James J. Murphy (Berkeley and Los Angeles: Univ. of California Press, 1978), pp. 3–24. I am grateful to Norman Kretzmann for helping me to get started in these difficult questions.

2. See also Eugene Vance, "The Modernity of the Middle Ages in the Future: Remarks on a Recent Book," *Romanic Review* 64 (1973), pp. 140–51; and Vance, "A Coda: Modern Medievalism and the Understanding of Understanding," *New Literary History* 10 (1978–1979), pp. 377–83.

3. Richard McKeon, "The Organization of Sciences and the Relations of Cultures in the Twelfth and Thirteenth Centuries," in *The Cultural Context of Medieval Learning*, ed. John Murdoch and Edith Sylla (Dordrecht: Reidel, 1975), p. 191.

4. Boethius, *De topicis differentiis*, Bk. 4, p. 80. References to Boethius are to Eleonore Stump's translation and are henceforth included in my text.

5. Petrus Abelardus, *De Dialectica*, ed. L. M. De Rijk (Assen: Van Gorcum, 1956), pp. 462–63: "Non est autem idem argumentum quod argumentatio. Id enim solum quod probat, argumentum dicimus. Totam vero complexionem probantis et probati argumentationem dicimus, ut totum syllogismum vel totum enthymema, ita scilicet ut in argumentatione argumentum quasi pars in toto contineatur."

6. Peter Haidu, *Aesthetic Distance in Chrétien de Troyes: Irony and Comedy in Cligès and Perceval* (Geneva: Droz, 1968).

7. Douglas Kelly, "La spécialité dans l'invention des topiques," in *Archéologie du signe*, ed. Lucie Brind'Amour and Eugene Vance (Toronto: Pontifical Institute of Mediaeval Studies, 1982), pp. 101–26; Kelly, "The Logic of the Imagination in Chrétien de Troyes," in *The Sower and His Seed*, ed. Pickens, pp. 9–30. In the latter article, Kelly evokes the need for a thorough study of topical theory with regard to rhetorical theory (p. 12). As I hope to demonstrate by this study, it is not in rhetoric itself, but in dialectics, that the most lucid and thorough articulation of topical theory may be found. I am convinced, moreover, that Chrétien was sufficiently familiar with the rudiments of dialectics (hence, of topical theory) to have transcended the very limited boundaries of topical theory as they are manifested in rhetorical theory of his time.

8. Matthieu de Vendôme, *Ars Versificatoria*, in *Les Arts poétiques du XIIe et du XIIIe siècle*, ed. Edmond Faral (Paris: Champion, 1924, reprint 1962), p. 143.

9. "Maximae propositiones illac dicuntur (regulae) quae, multarum consequentiarum sensus contenentes, communem inferentiae modum secundum vim eiusdem habitudinis demonstrant" (*Dialectica*, p. 310).

10. Boethius defines the enthymeme as "an imperfect syllogism, that is, discourse in which the precipitous conclusion is derived without all the propositions having been laid down beforehand, as when someone says 'man is an animal; therefore he is a substance,' he omits the other proposition, 'Every animal is a substance' " (*De topicis differentiis*, Bk. 4, p. 80).

11. St. Augustine, *De doctrina christiana* 2.1.1, trans. D. W. Robertson, Jr., under the title *On Christian Doctrine* (New York: Liberal Arts Press, 1950), p. 34.

Chapter 5. *Si est homo, est animal*

1. Alice M. Colby, *The Portrait in Twelfth-Century French Literature: An Example of the Stylistic Originality of Chrétien de Troyes* (Geneva: Droz, 1965).

2. While Boethius and Abelard considered dialectic to be essentially a process of question and answer, it is clear that the pragmatic history of medieval logic may in fact be described as the elaboration of a properly *textual* logic that is distinct from the context of the dialectical *disputatio*. See Alain de Libera, "Textualité logique et forme summuliste," and Thomas Maloney, "The *Summulae dialectices* of Roger Bacon and the Summulist Form," in *Archéologie du signe*, ed. Lucie Brind'Amour and Eugene Vance (Toronto: Pontifical Institute of Mediaeval Studies, 1980), pp. 213–34, 235–50.

3. Virgil, *Georgicon* 3. 215–23, in *P. Vergili Maronis, Opera*, ed. F. A. Hirtzel, (Oxford: Clarendon Press, 1900). See also Michael C. J. Putnam, *Virgil's Poem of the Earth: Studies in the Georgics* (Princeton: Princeton Univ. Press, 1979); and Eugene Vance, "Sylvia's Pet Stag: Wildness and Domesticity in Virgil's Aeneid," *Arethusa* 14 (1981), pp. 127–38.

4. The theme of the tripartition of the soul is amply expressed in Plato's *Phaedrus*, which was a major source of medieval platonism; see also Aristotle, *De anima* 3.10. 820–25; St. Augustine, *De libero arbitrio* 1.4.9. See Thomas on Aristotle, in *Aristotle's De anima in the Version of William of Moerbeke and the Commentary of St. Thomas*, trans. Foster and Humphries (New Haven: Yale Univ. Press, 1954), pp. 463–64.

5. St. Augustine expresses this hierarchy well in *On Free Will*: Human beings, he says, have much in common not only with lower animals, but also with plants and fortify themselves. Like animals, humans are also sensible: they see, hear, feel, touch, and have a sense of smell. "By our genus," Augustine writes, "we have much in common with brutes (*belluis*); moreover, to seek (*appetere*) the pleasures of the body and to avoid harm are the whole activity of bestial life" (1.8.18). Yet humans have in addition certain traits that are proper only to their species, such as being capable of laughter, as loving praise and glory, and as being rational. Reason alone, however, is the unique source of human superiority over all other species of the genus animal, though by "reason" Augustine means far more than the government of brute passion (emblematized in 1.9.19 by the figure of the wild animal tamer): it is wisdom (*sapientia*), or the love of spiritual things. (*De libero arbitrio, Patrologiae Latinae* 32. col. 1221–1303. I have used the text and French translation by F. J. Thonnard, *Oeuvres de Saint Augustin*, Bibliothèque Augustinienne, 1ère série, vol. 6 (Paris: Desclée de Brouwer, 1941). The English translation is my own.)

6. Aristotle, *Politics* 3.4, trans. Benjamin Jowett, in *Introduction to Aristotle*, ed. Richard McKeon (New York: Random House, 1947), pp. 583–86. See also Cicero, who following both Plato and Aristotle, writes, "But we must distinguish between different kinds of domination and subjection [*imperandi et serviendi*]. For the mind is said to rule over the body, and also over lust; but it rules over the body as a king governs his subjects, or a father his children, whereas it rules over lust as a master [*dominus*] rules his slaves, restraining it and breaking its power. So kings, commanders, magistrates, senators and popular assemblies govern citizens as the mind governs the body; but the master's restraint of his slaves is like the restraint exercised by the best part of the mind, the reason, over its own evil and weak elements, such as the lustful desires, anger, and the other disquieting emotions" (*De Republica* 3.25.37, trans., Clinton Walker Keyes (London: Heinemann; New York: Putnam's, 1928), pp. 213–15.

7. Alfarabi's *The Enumeration of the Sciences*, which contains ideas of political science drawn from Aristotle's politics, was heavily exploited by Dominicus Gundisalvi in his *De scientiis* in the middle of the twelfth century; Alfarabi was translated from the Arabic into Latin in Toledo about 1175. (*Medieval Political Philosophy: A Sourcebook*, ed. Ralph Lerner and Muhsin Mahdi [Glencoe, Ill.: The Free Press, 1963], p. 23)

8. St. Thomas, *De regimine principium*, ch. 10, in *Aquinas: Selected Political Writings*, ed. A. P. D'Entreves, trans. J. G. Dawson (Oxford: Blackwell, 1959), p. 59.

9. Richard Bernheimer, *Wild Men in the Middle Ages* (Cambridge, Mass.: Harvard Univ. Press, 1952), pp. 41–48; see also John Block Friedman, *The Monstrous Races in Medieval Art and Thought* (Cambridge, Mass.: Harvard Univ. Press, 1981).

10. For example, in *De Republica* 1.38.60, Cicero relishes the example of the statesman Archytas of Tarentum who refused to flog a certain slave to death, hardly because the slave did not deserve it, but because he would have flogged the slave in anger. In another work, his *De officiis* 1.25.89, Cicero censures all anger in the administration of justice: "In administering punishment it is above all necessary to allow no trace of anger. For if anyone proceeds in a passion to inflict punishment, he will never observe that happy mean which lies between excess and defect. This doctrine of the mean is approved by the Peripatetics—and wisely approved, if only they did not speak in praise of anger and tell us that it is a gift bestowed on us by Nature for a good purpose. But, in reality, anger is in every circumstances to be eradicated" (trans. Walter Miller. Loeb Classical Library, 1961, p. 91).

11. St. Augustine, *On the Trinity* 12.11, trans. A. W. Haddan, in *The Basic Writings of St. Augustine*, ed. Whitney Oates (New York: Random House, 1948), vol. 2, p. 818.

12. Erich Auerbach, *Literary Language and Its Public in Late Latin Antiquity and in the Middle Ages* (New York: Pantheon Books, 1965), pp. 66–81.

13. Aristotle, *Nicomachean Ethics* 2.7, trans. W. D. Ross, in *Introduction to Aristotle*, ed. Richard McKeon (New York: Random House, 1947), p. 343.

14. Jean Frappier, *Chrétien de Troyes* (Paris: Hatier, 1957), 150.

15. Aristotle, *Politics* 1.2, p. 556.

16. Michael C. J. Putnam, trans., *The Poetry of the* Aeneid (Cambridge: Harvard Univ. Press, 1965), p. 59.

17. Norbert Luyten, O.P., "Matter as Potency," in *The Concept of Matter in Greek and Medieval Philosophy*, ed. Ernan McMullin (South Bend: Univ. of Notre Dame Press, 1963), p. 102.

18. Bernard Sylvester, *Cosmographia*, trans. Winthrop Wetherbee, in *The Cosmographia of Bernardus Sylvestris* (New York: Columbia Univ. Press, 1973), p. 67. Wetherbee believes that the Latin *Silva* and the Greek *Hyle* are used interchangeably in Bernard's poem, but Brian Stock, *Myth and Science in the Twelfth Century* (Princeton: Princeton Univ. Press, 1972) believes that there are semantic differences between the terms: "*Silva* is much more involved than *hyle* in the moral allegory through which a new and better universe is to be formed. In this descriptions, Bernard points out that *silva* is to be refined into a more cultivated visage for the world while *hyle* represents the eternal source of matter which reproduces itself. In 1.1, it is *silva*, not *hyle*, which is associated with the image of a better form for *mundus*; it is she who is cut off from her own perfection and who longs to be reborn; it is she whom the infant cosmos thanks for being no worse off than it is. In 1.2, a slightly different, though no less allegorical portrait of matter is found. *Hyle*, at least to some extent, is said to be more stable than *silva*. She rests motionless, though surrounded by motion, and passionless, neither good nor evil in herself" (pp. 100–101). If Stock is right, perhaps the dialogue between the unchangeable man-beast and the more perfectable Calogrenant corresponds, at least in part, with what Stock calls Bernard's portrayal, in *Silva* and *Hyle* of "resonating, interdependant forms of the same reality" (p. 101).

19. On the implicit comparison between the poet's creative power and God's see Stock, pp. 119–37; see also Wetherbee, *Platonism and Poetry* for many good insights into poetic and divine creative power as imagined in the twelfth century.

20. Aristotle, *Politics* 1.2: "But he who is unable to live in society or has no need to because he is sufficient for himself, must be either a beast or a god: he is no part of a state. A social instinct is implanted in all men by nature, and yet he who first founded the state was the greatest of benefac-

tors. For man, when perfected, is the best of animals, but, when separated from law and justice, he is the worst of all."

21. Thomas Aquinas, *Commentary on the Politics* 1.1.35, trans. Ernest L. Fortin and Peter D. O'Neill, in *Medieval Political Philosophy* (Glencoe, Ill.: The Free Press, 1963), p. 310.

22. Georges Duby, *L'Economie rurale et la vie des campagnes dans l'Occident médiéval,* vol. 1 (Paris: Aubier, 1962), p. 146.

23. On the primacy of bread in the alimentary system of the Middle Ages, see Duby, *L'Economie rurale,* vol. 1, pp. 140–41.

24. Aristotle, *Politics* 1.2, p. 557: "A social instinct is planted in all men by nature, and yet he who first founded the state was the greatest of benefactors. For man, when perfected, is the best of animals, but, when separated from law and justice, he is the worst of all; since armed injustice is the more dangerous, and he is equipped at birth with arms, meant to be used by intelligence and virtue, which he may use for the worst ends. Wherefore if he have no virtue, he is the most unholy and the most savage of animals, and the most full of lust and gluttony."

25. Chrétien's narrative reflects, here, major developments in the economy of his century that implicated not only the secular community, but also the eccelesiastical and monastic communities. See Georges Duby, "Le budget de l'abbaye de Cluny entre 1080 et 1155: Economie domaniale et économie monétaire," *Annales: Economies Sociétés, Civilisations* 7 (1952), pp. 155–71; reprinted in *Hommes et structures du moyen-âge* (The Hauge and Paris: Mouton, 1973), pp. 61–82; see also Duby, *Guerriers et paysans* (Paris: Gallimard, 1973), pp. 280–300.

26. Emanuel J. Mickel, Jr., "Theme and Narrative Structure in *Guillaume d'Angleterre,*" in *The Sower and His Seed,* ed. Pickens, p. 58.

27. Elizabeth Chapin, *Les Villes de foires de Champagne des origines au début du XIVe siècle* (Paris: Champion, 1937); R. Bautier, "Les foires de Champagne. Recherches sur une évolution historique," in *La foire,* Receuils de la Société Jean Bodin, vol. 5 (Brussels: Editions de la librairie encyclopédique 1953), pp. 97–147; Duby, *Guerriers et paysans,* p. 280; Henri Dubois, "Le commerce et les foires au temps de Philippe Auguste," in *La France de Philippe auguste. Le temps des mutations,* ed. Robert-Henri Bautier (Paris: Editions du C. N. R. S., 1982), pp. 689–709.

28. Peter Haidu, "The Hermit's Pottage: Deconstruction and History in *Yvain,*" in *The Sower and His Seed,* ed. Pickens, p. 134.

29. Jean Becquet, "Erémistime et hérésie au moyen-âge, in *Hérésies et sociétés dans l'Europe pré-industrielle, Xie–XVIIIe siècles* (Paris: Ecole pratique des hautes études, 1964), pp. 139–45.

30. Jean Leclercq, "L'érémitisme en occident jusqu'à l'an mille," in *L'eremitismo in occidente nei secoil XIe XII,* ed. Cinzio Violante and Cosimo Damiano Fonseca, Pubblicazioni dell'Universita cattolica del sacro cuore, Serie terza, varia 4 (Milan: Società editrice vita e pensiero, 1965), pp. 27–44.

31. Bernard Bligny, "L'érémitisme et les chartreux," in *L'eremitismo in occidente,* pp. 248–70.

32. Jean Leclercq, "Le poème de Payen Bolotin contre les faux ermites," *Revue bénédictine* 67 (1957), pp. 52–86, especially p. 68.

33. Léopold Génicot, "L'érémitisme du XIe 5. dans son contexte économique et social," *L'eremetismo in occidente,* pp. 57, 61; Jean Becquet, "L'érémitisme clérical et laïc dans l'ouest de la France," in *L'eremitismo in occidente,* pp. 187–88.

34. Leclercq, "L'érémitisme en occident," p. 27–44.

35. J. G. Sikes, *Peter Abailard* (Cambridge: Cambridge Univ. Press, 1932), p. 20; Jean Jolivet, *Abélard* (Paris: Seghers, 1969), pp. 30–31.

36. Duby, *Guerriers et paysans,* p. 280.

37. R. Howard Bloch, "Merlin and the Modes of Medieval Legal Meaning," in *Archéologie du signe,* p. 127.

38. Jacques Le Goff, *La Naissance du Purgatoire* (Paris: Gallimard, 1981), p. 227.

39. Claude Lévesque and Christie V. McDonald, eds., *L'Oreille de l'autre: textes et débats avec Jacques Derrida* (Montréal: VLB Editeur, 1982), p. 118.

Chapter 6. From Man-Beast to Lion-Knight: Difference, Kind, and Emblem

1. Aristotle, speaking of the vegetative basis of all animate beings says, "Now excellence of this seems to be common to all species and not specifically human; for this part of faculty seems to function most in sleep, while goodness and badness are least manifest in sleep (whence comes the saying that the happy are no better off than the wretched for half of their lives; and this happens naturally enough, since sleep is an inactivity of the soul in that respect in which it is called good or bad)" (*Nichomachean Ethics* 1.13, trans. W. D. E. Ross, in *Introduction to Aristotle*, ed. Richard McKeon (New York: Random House, 1947), p. 309.

2. Mark Shell, *The Economy of Literature* (Baltimore: Johns Hopkins Univ. Press, 1978), p. 64.

3. Cf. Eugene Vance, "Le combat érotique chez Chrétien de Troyes," *Poétique* 12 (1972), pp. 544–71; also Vance, "Signs of the City: Medieval Poetry as Detour," *New Literary History* 4 (1972–73), pp. 557–74.

4. Virgil, *Aeneid* 10.723–29; in *P. Vergili Maronis Opera*, ed. F. A. Hirtzel (Oxford: Clarendon Press, 1900); trans. L. R. Lind, *Virgil's Aenid* (Bloomington: Indiana Univ. Press, 1962).

5. Cf. Jean Charles Payen, "L'enracinement folklorique du roman arthurien," *Travaux de linguistique et de litterature* 16 (1978), pp. 427–37.

6. Julian Harris, "The Role of the Lion in Chrétien de Troyes' *Yvain*," *PMLA* 64 (1949), pp. 1143–63.

7. Porphyry, *Isagoge*, trans. Edward W. Warren (Toronto: Pontifical Institute of Medieval Studies, 1975), p. 43.

8. Eleonore Stump, "Differentia and the Porphyrian Tree," in *Boethius's De topicis differentiis*, p. 239.

9. Uberto Eco, *Semiotics and the Philosophy of Language* (Bloomington: Indiana Univ. Press, 1984), p. 64.

10. Abelard, *Super Porphyrium*, ed. Mario Dal Pra, in *Scritti filosofici* (Milan: Fratelli Bocca, 1954), p. 17.

11. T. H. White, trans. *The Bestiary: A Book of Beasts* (New York: G. P. Putnam's Sons, 1954), pp. 7–11.

12. Sigmund Freud, "The Uncanny," in *Collected Papers*, vol. 4, trans. Joan Rivers (London: The Hogarth Press, 1957), p. 394.

13. John Bloch Freidman, *The Monstrous Races in Medieval Art and Thought* (Cambridge: Harvard Univ. Press, 1981), p. 122.

14. R. Howard Bloch, *Etymologies and Genealogies: A Literary Anthropology of the French Middle Ages* (Chicago: Univ. of Chicago Press, 1983), pp. 91–92.

15. Claude Gandelman, "The Metastability of Signs / Metastability as Sign," *Semiotica* 28 (1979), p. 83.

16. *Collected Papers of Charles Sanders Peirce*, ed. Charles Hartshorne and Paul Weiss (Cambridge, Mass.: Harvard Univ. Press, 1931–1935), vol. 2, par. 2.

17. Gerard J. Brault, *Early Blazon: Heraldic Terminology in the Twelfth and Thirteenth Centuries With Special Reference to Arthurian Literature* (Oxford: Clarendon Press, 1972), p. 28. See also Michel Pastoreau, *Traité d'héraldique*, (Paris: Picard, 1979), pp. 21–65.

18. *Collected Papers of Charles Sanders Peirce*, vol. 2, par. 249: "A *Symbol* is a sign that refers to the Object that it denotes by virtue of a law, usually an association of general ideas, which operates to cause the symbol to be interpreted by referring to that Object." Peirce's use of the word "symbol" is very different and opposed to the traditional romantic sense of that term, as conveyed by Coleridge and C. S. Lewis.

19. St. Augustine, *De ordine* 2.12.36, trans. Robert P. Russell, under the title *Divine Providence*

and the Problem of Evil: A Translation of St. Augustine's De Ordine (New York: Cosmopolitain Science and Art Service, Co., 1942), p. 141.

20. John F. Benton, "Written Records and the Development of Systematic Feudal Relations" (Paper presented at the conference, "Language and History in the Middle Ages," Centre for Medieval Studies, University of Toronto, November 6–7, 1981).

21. Michel Pastoureau, *Les armoiries*, Typologie des sources due moyen-âge occidental, fasc. 20 (Turnhout: Brépols, 1976), p. 46.

22. For a recent study of the relationship between genealogy, romance, and heraldry, see R. Howard Bloch, *Etymologies and Genealogies: A Literary Anthropology of the French Middle Ages* (Chicago: Univ. of Chicago Press, 1983), especially pp. 64–91. See also L. Genicot, *Les Généalogies*, Typologie des sources ou moyen-âge occidental, fasc. 15 (Turnhout: Brépols, 1975).

23. Alexandre Leupin, *Le Graal et la littérature* (Lausanne: L'Age de l'homme, 1982). Leupin's book addresses many questions raised by Bloch concerning the relationship between kinship and narrative, but he stresses, rather, principles of false lineage and incest as hidden motors of romance narrative.

24. Claude Lévi-Strauss, *Le totémisme aujourd'hui* (Paris: Presses Universitaires de France, 1962), p. 37.

25. "Si nomen est pars orationis, ergo est pars existens in oracione. Ergo si non est pars existens in oracione, non est nomen. Ergo nisi sit oratio non est nomen." in L. M. De Rijk, *Logica Modernorum: A Contribution to the History of Early Terminist Logic* (Assen: Van Gorcum, 1967), vol. 2, pt. 1, p. 245.

26. Brian Stock, *The Implications of Literacy: Written Language and Models of Interpretation in the Eleventh and Twelfth Centuries* (Princeton: Princeton Univ. Press, 1983), pp. 88–240.

27. Rodney Dennys, *The Heraldic Imagination* (London: Barrie and Jenkins, 1975), p. 133.

Index

Index

Theory and History of Literature

Eugene Vance is a professor of French and comparative literature at Emory University in Atlanta, Georgia. He is the author of *Reading the Song of Roland* and *Marvelous Signals: Poetics and Sign Theory in the Middle Ages*, and principal editor of the Regents Studies in Medieval Culture at the University of Nebraska Press.

Wlad Godzich is director of the Center for Humanistic Studies at the University of Minnesota and co-editor of the series Theory and History of Literature.